ENDS

Steve Swanson's life has always been dedicated to music, but music took on new meaning for him through the transforming work of Jesus. He has been forever changed by the privilege to worship. I have been in countless meetings where Steve has led and have experienced firsthand the wonder of his unique gift. In his fascinating book, *Heaven's Symphony*, Steve reveals how creation interacts with and continuously worships its creator. This book is an invitation to join in. Backed by years of experience, it is practical for worship leaders and worshipers alike. *Heaven's Symphony* is sure to mark your life for good.

BILL JOHNSON
Bethel Church, Redding, CA
Author of *When Heaven Invades Earth* and
Hosting the Presence

It is my great joy and privilege to endorse Steve Swanson's book *Heaven's Symphony*. I love worshiping with Steve—we always go so deep into the anointing and God's presence. The most important thing we can do is cultivate intimacy with Daddy God, all fruitfulness and everything good in our lives flow from this relationship. No one can give you deeper intimacy; the only way to get more oil is to stop for the One who is the One and spend time with Him in the secret place. God is searching the earth for those who will surrender everything to Him in this place, ones who will be holy-given, laid-down lovers. Steve is one who lives a life of pure worship on and off the stage. I pray that as you read you will learn about holy worship; but more than that, I pray that you will get hungry for more of God in your own life and worship Him with all that you are. He is worthy of it all.

HEIDI G. BAKER, PhD
Co-Founder and Director of Iris Global

I have had the privilege of knowing and working with Steve Swanson for a number of years. He is an incredible worship leader, skillful musician, and songwriter. He exemplifies Psalm 33:3. He consistently creates and sings a fresh new sound. He is skillful in his musicianship and releases joy in the middle of it all. In Steve's new book, *Heaven's Symphony*, we get to peer into his journey in worship. He brings us along as he encounters God and shares the keys he has found to sustain the presence of God throughout this journey of life. Much like King David chronicled his life through the Psalms, so has Steve invited us to glimpse into his life. He writes of his conversations with God and his passion to release the songs, the sounds, and the rhythms of Heaven to the earth. I feel as if desire, hunger, and encounter are released to the reader on every page. This is not a book for worshipers alone, though they will benefit greatly, it's for everyone who hungers for a deeper walk in God, a greater desire for God, and for those wanting to experience God in every place and in every season.

JULIE MEYER
International House of Prayer
Kansas City, Missouri

The psalmist tells us that those who know the "joyful sound" are truly blessed. All of creation is a song. In fact, Leonard Sweet, one of the foremost theologians in the Western world, has often said, "In the beginning was the Song, and the Song was with God, and the Song was God," in paraphrasing logos in John 1:1. I spent twenty-six years of my personal journey, from the time I was five years of age, studying the keyboard and then earning an undergraduate degree in Music Theory and Composition and Performance, with a minor in Theology. I didn't fully realize in those earlier days the significance of the connection between sound, music, and God Himself. Mastery in any field of discipline takes time. Mastery in sound is an ongoing journey of destiny for a musician and a psalmist. Steve Swanson is one of those rare eagles in the world of worship and psalmody who transforms an atmosphere the moment he lifts his voice and his hands dance on the keyboards setting before him. His insight into the transforming power of sound is so life-giving that anyone who is in his presence experiences both Steve and the Creator as together they harmonize the sounds of Heaven and earth. Steve's first book is in your hand, and it is a worthwhile read. Take time to experience the experience of the power of sound, worship, and the King of Song Himself, in this fabulous journey entitled *Heaven's Symphony*.

BISHOP MARK J. CHIRONNA, MA, PhD

I first heard Steve Swanson's music as a pastor looking for a new worship leader. After listening to his CD, I turned to my wife in amazement and declared, "He is playing my heart." Over the next several years my appreciation for Steve's talent and his heart increased. After years of friendship, Steve has again stunned me with the brilliance and anointing of his work. In *Heaven's Symphony*, Steve brings the poetry of his songs and his heart for worship to the written pages. Through the sharing of his story and the secrets of entering God's presence, you will be drawn into worship and an insatiable desire to join the celestial symphony.

Dr. Tom Jones
Executive Director
Global Awakening

HEAVEN'S SYMPHONY

HEAVEN'S SYMPHONY

YOUR INVITATION TO UNLOCKING
DIVINE ENCOUNTERS THROUGH WORSHIP

STEVE SWANSON

DESTINY IMAGE® PUBLISHERS, INC.

P.O. Box 310, Shippensburg, PA 17257-0310

"Promoting Inspired Lives."

This book and all other Destiny Image and Destiny Image Fiction books are available at Christian bookstores and distributors worldwide.

For more information on foreign distributors, call 717-532-3040.

Reach us on the Internet: www.destinyimage.com.

Cover Design by: River Publishing & Media Ltd.

ISBN 13 TP: 978-0-7684-0539-2

ISBN 13 Ebook: 978-0-7684-0540-8

For Worldwide Distribution, Printed in the U.S.A.

1 2 3 4 5 6 7 8 / 19 18 17 16 15

DEDICATION

This book is dedicated to my Friend and Savior, Jesus, who loves me unconditionally.

Also to my wife, Lisa, who is with me every step of the journey. I love you!

ACKNOWLEDGMENTS

Special thanks to: Lisa, Jordan, and Jacob Swanson; Ronald and Theo Sittser (Mom and Dad); Randy Clark; Tom Jones; Rachel K. Austin; Kent Henry; Tim and Deborah Greenidge; JoAnn McFatter; and the editors and staff at Destiny Image Publishers. Thank you!

Music is the harmonious voice of creation;
an echo of the invisible world.

—Giuseppe Mazzini

CONTENTS

FOREWORD

Heaven's Symphony should be required reading for every worship leader, every member of a worship team or choir, every pastor, all elders and deacons, and all members of church boards, councils, or sessions. In fact, it should be read by all worshipers and all believers. There is such wisdom in Steve Swanson's new book, *Heaven's Symphony*. Wisdom for worship leaders and wisdom for pastors in particular. I believe *Heaven's Symphony* could be used to bring a greater clarity of purpose and philosophy of ministry. If a traditional church choir would read it together at the same time and discuss the chapters, it would bring a greater sense of purpose to the choir. If a nontraditional praise team did the same, it would produce not only a greater sense of purpose, but also faith for a greater release of God's glory and power in the church congregation.

I found *Heaven's Symphony* to be an amazing insight into worship. Not since 1984 when I read Jack Taylor's *Hallelujah Factor* have I been so impressed with a book dedicated to thanksgiving, praise, and worship—all with the great desire to experience Him and His glory. However, *Heaven's Symphony* goes past the meaning of the words associated with thanksgiving, praise, and worship. It offers practical instruction to worship leaders and lays the path for pastors to understand that they are not looking for a "song leader," rather they are looking for a "worship leader."

I believe that even if a pastor cannot lead worship, the insight gained from this book will help the pastor to disciple a worship leader in matters of the heart and the goal of worship. Thirty years ago I received a similar insight into worship as I was about to leave the denomination I had been raised in to become one of the thirty leaders in the Vineyard movement. I received this insight by listening to a tape by John Wimber[1] about worship. Steve Swanson would make John happy, building upon his ceiling to take the Church higher and farther in God.

If the leadership of local churches read this book and digest its truths (and there are many), then I believe the Church as a whole will begin to see more conversions, more backsliders come home, more healings, and more miracles. There will be more joy in the presence of the Lord.

I encourage you to buy this book, read it, meditate on its insights and truths, and make any adjustments in your life that the Holy Spirit speaks to you. Even if you are a worship leader, on a worship team, a member of a choir, or a pastor, you should read this book. Do not put it on a shelf to read at a more convenient time, read it now. Why? Because Steve's message is a *now* message.

My desire is that each reader will have an experience like Steve had when he was touched by the power and glory of God—when his ears were opened to hear *Heaven's Symphony*.

Randy Clark
www.globalawakening.com

ENDNOTE

1. John Wimber, "The Five Phase Worship Model" © Equipping the Saints, Vol. 1, No. 1. Used with permission. Renewal Journal #6 (1995:2), Brisbane, Australia, 3-7. http://www.renewaljournal.com. Reproduction permitted with copyright intact with text.

PREFACE

There are moments in one's life that set the course of destiny. These "God Encounters" happen suddenly and something changes, all of a sudden we can't look or hear things the same way. There has been a shift of perspective. It's during those times when a piece of Heaven opens up and allows us to peer inside an eternal reality.

So what do we do with these moments? My hope, as you read this book, is that you will be able to apply these divine encounters to your life, and have a better understanding of how to access these realms of Heaven and release them on the earth. After reading *Heaven's Symphony*, I pray that you will have a heightened awareness of the constant worship going on all around you both in Heaven and on the earth. I trust that the testimonies of my life, encounters, and practical applications will open these realms for you; and even more, that they will entice you to discover more about God and His glory, leading you into your own encounters with Him. It can happen in an instant! Your "suddenly" is right around the corner!

JOINING THE
SYMPHONY

I experience God in sounds. I hear Him in the changing direction of the winds, in the gentle babble of a lazy stream, and in the hush of a sleeping child's breath. I hear Him in the celebration of worship, in the instruments I play, and in the heavenly background music of my life. His voice is heard in notes and tones and whistles and swooshes.

I suppose other people experience God in ways different from mine. The artist sees Him in colors, shapes, visual contrasts, and dimensions; he experiences God through his eyes. The mathematician perceives God's activity in the precision and fluidity of measurements, movements, forces, proportions, and vectors. The writer senses Him in the poetry of perfectly selected words. God crafted me as a musician, so I hear him in sounds. Perhaps all of us experience Him in each of these ways and other ways we may not even understand—our distinct personalities, talents, and destinies allow us to sense the different colors of His activity and presence uniquely. We all hear and contribute to different parts of God's symphony. But I love that He speaks to me in sounds.

I've known from a very early age that music was to be my life. I started playing piano before my hands were large enough to span an octave. I could write notes before I could scrawl my name; and singing or making noise with my mouth or any other source that happened to be available, came more naturally to me than talking. Through music, I've experienced my most heartbreaking moments as well as the joys of breakthrough and victory. There were times I followed music more than I followed the God who gave me the ears and creativity to hear it. The choices I've made along the journey have shaped me into the man I am today.

Life is full of choices. God, in His love for us, granted us free will. We are free to choose Him and His path for our lives. We are equally free to choose to follow our own brokenness away from Him. Our lives are defined by the choices we make, the big ones and the seemingly innocuous little ones that occur daily. For every action there is a reaction. Every choice has its consequences.

WHAT IF...

I've often wondered, *What if.* What if I had chosen B instead of A at time Z? Would I still be where I am today?

Or would I be in some parallel universe somewhere doing something completely different? What if I hadn't chosen to accept that position as a worship leader in a large Portland church in my 30s? What if I hadn't heeded that dream God gave me in 1999?

I believe God has a plan for our lives. When we choose to dedicate our lives to the Lord, I believe He lays out the steps of our lives before us. They are like footprints in the sand of our life history and destiny. Sometimes we prophetically receive a glimpse of where that path is leading us. At other times we have to trust God in our nearsightedness to walk with us step by step by step. We can choose to walk in those footprints, or we can choose to stray onto our own paths. When we stay on the path God has for us, we end up where He wants us—in the intersection of our destiny and His divine providence, I call it convergence. It's that time in your life when you realize everything has come together and there you are in the center of His will.

All of us occasionally take side excursions. Sometimes we take intentional leaps away from God's design. Other times, we look up to His glorious face and He points out to us how we have slowly drifted off course. But God in His infinite wisdom knows our choices before we do. He knows how to readjust our path to bring us back to His original intent. So for each of our actions, in essence, there is a reaction by the Spirit that guides us back on course. Suddenly we are converging back into destiny.

The joy comes in the journey. Destiny is a process, not necessarily a destination. It is not promised to us that we will live in our full destiny, but we are promised that God will be with us on every detour, eager to set us back on track. Our joy comes in our nearness to Him.

While we do have many choices, there are some things that happen along the journey that we don't have any choice about. There are God moments—divine encounters—that simply happen to us. He radically reveals Himself and His desires to us. After these encounters, the choice is ours what to do with them. These encounters are the reaction of Heaven's guidance system, the spiritual GPS. There are times when divine encounters place us back on track. Other times, we are already in the right place, doing the right things, when that divine encounter propels us forward in an unexpected direction. It seems like a change in course, but it's directly in the path God has planned all along. Unbeknownst to us, He was waiting for the perfect time in our journey to launch us forward in order to generate the greatest impact for His kingdom.

TRUST AND OBEY

Obedience is the key to staying in God's presence during the journey He has set before us. Obedience means placing more faith in God's provision, goodness, and wisdom than in our own understanding and fear. Proverbs 3:5-6 instructs us, "Trust in the Lord with all your heart, and lean not on your own understanding; in all your ways acknowledge Him, and He shall direct your paths."

Obedience requires sacrifice. Are you willing to lay down everything for God? Is His presence worth the sacrifice of trusting Him with your future, your family, your heart? Are you willing to say, "God, wherever You want me to go, that's where I'll go, regardless of what it costs me"? Are you willing to lay down everything you know to move across the country when God leads you? Are you willing to blaze a trail for God when you look back and no one else is following? Are you willing to persevere in faith after losing someone you have sung and prayed over for two years, fully believing that they would rise up and be healed?

It's easy to trust God and obey when life is what you want it to be. It's harder to trust and obey when we, like Christ, must take up our crosses to follow Him. There is a price to pay for this life in Christ. No one said it would be easy. The anointing on our lives has to be refined just like oil. Refining requires fire along the way. The path to the finish line requires excursions through the crucible of sanctification.

We don't just arrive at the finish line. We are works in progress going through a process to run this race with excellence. First Corinthians 9:24 tells us, "Do you not know that those who run in a race all run, but one receives the prize? Run in such a way that you may obtain it." I hope to obtain the prize. The prize is God's presence as we run. The prize is Him saying, "Well done, good and faithful servant."

As we look back on our journey of obedience to God, we can see His guidance along the way. In hindsight,

I can see that there were many turns and kinks during my journey, and without them I wouldn't be where I am today. If I hadn't "accidentally" been in that place at that time, I wouldn't have been given the opportunity to make that critical shift. If I hadn't met that person who spoke that destiny word from God over my life, my perspective wouldn't have changed.

Obedience can be overthought. We can't be paralyzed with fear of missing God. I call it blind obedience—when you trust what you know in your spirit is the right thing to do, and the green light of grace says, "Go for it!" You need to trust God's ability to lead you more than you trust your ability to understand. Obedience is a journey in faith training, not a set of instructions to follow.

The same principle applies to leading worship. I don't want my mind to get in the way of the Spirit. In my desire to know what God is doing, I don't want to overthink trust. Trust, by its nature, relies on God's wisdom over our own. I desire to follow the lead of the Holy Spirit in full faith, knowing I'll reach His destination.

As we trust and obey, we find ourselves swept up in the symphony of this beautiful masterpiece God is crafting. Each believer brings different colors, sounds, and assets to the symphony. The symphony moves us and we help shape the sound as well. We are a combination God's creation joined in a mighty chorus of worship to Him. We join with the angels, elders, creatures, and all of creation to sing praises to our God.

So before you now are the pages of my life. Included are the stories of choices, obedience, sacrifice, and divine encounters that propelled me to the place God wanted me to be. By no means am I saying that I have arrived; but as I continue to follow, I find more of Him along the way—and that's a good thing. Also included are some practical tools and advice I have acquired in my journey as one who has the privilege of leading thousands into worship. My hope is that this book will be one of those divine encounter circumstances that launches you forward in your destiny as well. My prayer is that you enjoy the journey and join the symphony.

CHAPTER 1

YEARNING FOR FREEDOM

There is no freedom like the freedom experienced in worship. As I lift my voice, heart, and hands to love on this amazing, holy, wondrous God, I am enraptured by His presence. As I focus my full attention on Him, every shackle that binds me to earth loosens its hold. Every care, every uncertainty, every fear melts away. Nothing else matters but loving Jesus more, singing of His glory forever, and experiencing His tangible presence. There's no way to be more free than when I am free to worship my Creator. I love that freedom. But I haven't always experienced it.

I grew up in the church. I mean, quite literally, I grew up in the church. My parents were both ministers. Mom divorced my birth father when I was young then married this amazing guy who became Dad to me. I couldn't have asked for better parents. Dad pastored our church, which was literally one step outside our door. One minute I'm playing the piano in the house; thirty seconds later, I'm sitting on the front pew in the sanctuary.

Our church was a small, kingdom-minded Pentecostal church. It was all I ever knew, and I loved it. Dad would preach from his heart, never from notes. His favorite sermon topic was the kingdom of God, which was a cutting-edge message back in the late 1950s and 60s. He would deliver impassioned altar calls, and Mom would accent his preaching at the organ or piano as her notes accompanied everything that happened in the room. We would sing these great three-chord hymns and camp meeting-style songs. They riveted me with the truth of the Word and instilled messages of hope that linger even now.

I experienced so much freedom in that church. The Spirit would move, and I could feel God's presence. We would worship for hours with singing, dancing, and yes, even tambourines. As a kid I would lose myself in that place of worship. Nothing else mattered—no other cares or worries or thoughts of anything else but to bask in God's presence and enjoy His freedom.

That church is also where my musical talents found their first foothold. I started leading worship there when I was only eight years of age. That church environment gave me the freedom to grow from being a kid with some talent to a teen with above-average musical skills. The piano became a magical place where I met God and God met me.

Something changed, though, in my later years of high school. It was the mid-70s, and I found myself hanging out with the wrong kind of people. I began to backslide. From childhood, I had known that God's hand was on me and that He had a big calling for my life. I had received so many prophetic words as a young man telling me about the big plans God had for my life.

Looking back, as much as those words excited me, they also scared me. I wasn't just running from God, I was also running from who He called me to be. Slowly, that freedom I had known as a child was beginning to feel more like a burden I had to carry.

FREEDOM FADING

So I decided to stick with what I knew: music. I delved into it with a passion. The skills I had honed on a church piano were translated to a different scene. I started pursuing a career as a professional musician and kept myself busy playing in clubs, resorts, and restaurants. I sang and produced several commercial spots. I was a California Raisin! That was pretty cool—got a $20,000 paycheck for singing in the studio for twenty minutes. Easy money.

I was refining my musical skills, but I was also slowly sinking further into a pit of despair. I thought I was pursuing happiness. I thought I was climbing my way up to the big life. I got married young. Started gaining traction with my career. Cashed paychecks for doing what I loved and came natural to me. What more could I want from life, right?

The bubble burst when I was twenty-three years of age. I discovered my wife of two years was having an extramarital affair, and my life began to spin out of control. The downward spiral of darkness went from distress to depression to hopelessness to despondency.

What had happened to all that freedom I had experienced as a kid in that little church next door? Where was the joy? I couldn't even remember what that had once felt like, nonetheless try to find a way to recapture it. So I did the only thing I knew to do: just keep going one day at a time doing the music scene. More night clubs. More commercials. Did some spots for Nike, Toyota, and several other companies. Whatever paid the bills I'd do. Did radio spots for the Morning Zoo. More singing. More gigs. More clubs. More nothingness.

I did whatever I could to fill the ache. I may not have been fully aware of it at the time—in fact, I'm sure I wasn't—but there was also an ongoing rhythm singing the background template of my life. It was a symphony that I first began hearing as a child. It was the sound of the Spirit in that little Pentecostal church in my house. I couldn't escape it. Rather, God wouldn't let me escape Him.

BLACK-HOLE MOMENTS

The symphony continued, sometimes quietly, but eventually growing to a discordant static that I couldn't ignore.

I was searching for something. Searching for a way out of the night music scene. Searching for an escape from the hopelessness. Searching for a way back home. Searching for God.

I kept thinking, *There's got to be more than this. More than brawls in nightclubs and meaningless paychecks with entangling strings attached. More than this black hole of nonexistence I find myself in. All I've ever known is music, and I pursued it with every ounce of my being. But it left me here. Here in a tail spin into darkness so acute that I can't fathom a way out.*

It can be in those times—those black-hole moments when God seems so far away—when God actually has you right in the palm of His hand. Exactly where He wants you and perfectly in His care. He began dealing with my heart, though I'm certain I wasn't cognizant of His activity at the time. He was placing people, situations, and settings in my path that began to shape my journey. He knew what I didn't—that this divinely crafted path would lead me back to Him. It would lead me into the next dimension of His destiny for my life.

Destiny intersected my despair one day on a train while traveling with my new wife, Lisa. We were headed home to Portland, Oregon, from Los Angeles after I had completed a gig there. Our conversation turned to considering what we should do with our lives. The monotony was getting to her just as the hopelessness was swallowing me. We knew something had to give. We seemed to have finally come to that dead end in which forward is no longer an option, but any other direction is fraught with uncertainty.

We were seated in the restaurant car, and the crowded train made it impossible to eat and converse in private. As we talked, an interesting, peculiar lady with glistening blonde hair sat down at our table. It's not uncommon to eat meals with strangers on train cars, but on this particular occasion, I wasn't particularly in the mood for interaction.

Just as I was beginning to regret our seating choice, the lady looked me square in the eyes and said, "You're running from God. He's got a call on your life and a marvelous plan for you. But you're running from Him and running from the call." Then she rose from her seat at the dinner table and walked out the door. She seemed to have disappeared as suddenly as she had arrived, and her departure was as startling as her acute message.

It was as if my whole life was derailed in that moment. I was on one set of tracks pursuing happiness in my musical career when God's switchboard pulled an unexpected lever and I found myself diverging onto a new set of tracks. I knew where the old tracks were supposed to lead, but this track was unknown to me—wonderfully, hopefully, finally unknown. I didn't know what changes needed to be made in my life, but I knew they were going to be significant, and I knew they led me out of bondage and back to freedom with God.

I didn't know where to go next, but God did. He brought an amazing friend into my life named Timothy. He was a big, boisterous guy with a huge family—thirteen kids and lots of cousins and extended family always around him. He sang in a gospel choir, and I really liked him. He made my heart hope again. When I was drowning in my confusion, Timothy would point me back to God. His words and actions would shift my perspective back to God's goodness, provision, and faithfulness. I would complain that I didn't know which way to go, and Timothy would remind me that God is our light. I didn't know how to pull out of my depressed state—and Timothy would remind me that God is our hope. I didn't know how to be a husband, a musician, a child of God—and Timothy would remind me that God shows the way. Moment after moment, day after day, God was using Timothy to bring me back into the joy of a relationship with Him.

A GLORIOUS RETURN

Timothy's sister, Deborah, was a worship pastor at a great church; she knew of me and the calling on my life and invited me to play keyboards for a night of worship with their amazing gospel choir. God was setting me up for a glorious return! If you want to see me in a puddle at the altar, just play me a song with a great gospel choir and I'm undone. There's something about the sound of a gospel choir, the tenors singing at full tilt, the altos filling the void, and the sopranos just flat out bringing it! I imagine the symphony of Heaven is filled with voices like that!

I remember that night of worship, simply because I couldn't read the charts through my tears—they were tears of joy, tears of redemption. It was as if God had salvaged a wreck from the junk heap and began to perform CPR on my heart. After the meeting the whole choir gathered around me and began to pray for a refilling of the Holy Spirit; they kept saying, "like a mighty rushing wind, like a mighty rushing wind." Suddenly, I could feel the wind again and it was renewing my spirit!

One day Timothy called me with an idea. "Hey, Steve! My church needs a new worship pastor. We need help down here, and you're a great musician. Why don't you apply for the job?"

A worship pastor? It had been years since I had stepped into a church, not to mention led worship in a church. I really didn't know anything about how to lead worship except at Mom and Dad's place. I recorded a couple of Christian albums and I had spent some time in youth ministry years ago, so I knew a little about church ministry life, but I had never been on a church staff. Besides, that seemed like a lifetime ago.

What made it worse, I knew about Timothy's church—a large, denominational, Pentecostal church. It was much bigger than the living room church I had grown up in, and leading worship for twenty is a totally different story from leading the 1,500 who regularly attended Timothy's church. It required a completely different skill set from the one I had at the time.

Despite all my objections, I knew something deep inside. God had switched the tracks. The course I had been on couldn't fulfill me anymore. Something drastically different had to happen in my life, and this church fit that description. I wasn't quite ready to apply for the job, but I decided to at least visit the church one Sunday.

It didn't take long for me to realize what Timothy meant when he said the church needed help with their music. They were missing key changes, their vocal harmonies were way off pitch, and their tempo was a mess. But it was something else entirely that struck me profoundly. It wasn't the music—it was the message the pastor was preaching.

The sermon topic was John 9:4, "I must work the works of him that sent me while it is day; the night cometh, when no man can work" (KJV). The phrase "while it is day" was repeated over and over—whether in my spirit or from the pulpit I couldn't tell. "While it is day." That was all I could hear. I could tell that Lisa, who was sitting beside me, was hearing the same thing. We looked at each other, and all of a sudden everything seemed so clear. I needed to pursue God, develop my music, and enjoy my life "while it is day." No more nightclubs. No more restaurants and resorts. No more commercials with their big paychecks and fifteen seconds of fame. I had to lay it all down while it was day and run hard after God. I didn't know what it all meant or how to walk it out, but I knew the course of my life had been radically changed.

A short time later, God gave me a dream one night. In the dream, I heard God's audible voice saying, "I am your God. I will show you the path to follow. It's in Psalm 9:10." When I woke, the dream felt so real, but I didn't know what the dream meant, nor did I know what Psalm 9:10

said. So I pulled out my dusty Bible and turned to Psalm 9:10, "And those who know Your name will put their trust in You; for You, Lord, have not forsaken those who seek You." It was a confirmation to me—not just from the Spirit but also from the Word—that I needed to trust God. To trust this new track He had placed me on. It was one of those destiny moments in which I knew I was perfectly in the love and will of God. All the doubts and uncertainties fell away as I soaked in the assurance of knowing His presence, His guidance, and His love.

I didn't know much, but I knew I at least needed to compile a resume to apply for the worship- leading position at Timothy's church. But what would I put on the resume that would impress a pastor of a 1,500-member church? Led worship as a child at a tiny house church? Was a singing California Raisin? Played the midnight slot in the club scene? Partially attended college? I presented my vapid past in the most meaningful way possible, and somehow I managed to put something on paper that seemed halfway presentable.

Remarkably, I was called in for an interview. The pastor sat across from me at a large desk as he eyed through my resume. I, however, was having trouble eyeing anything because tears were streaming down my face. Through the entire interview, my heart was overwhelmed as I couldn't hold back the tears anymore. Years of searching for fulfillment in the least fulfilling places had worn a hole into my soul that seemed ready to engulf me. Yet at the same time,

I could tangibly sense God's presence, His acceptance, and His guidance in bringing me to this church.

"I JUST WANT GOD TO USE ME"

Despite my blubbering initial meeting—the only thing I could say was, "I just want God to use me"—the pastor offered me the opportunity to try out for the position before the church board by being a guest worship leader one Sunday. I jumped at the opportunity. There's more to that story that I will tell later, but long story short, I was eventually offered the job.

I was simultaneously ecstatic and overwhelmed. This unique church offered me lots of opportunities to stretch and grow. I had inherited a hodge-podge of musicians I had to somehow wrangle together to make some sort of musical sense. There was a very interesting organ. It sounded more like a pizza parlor organ than a Crystal Cathedral masterpiece. The strangest sounds would come out of that instrument. However, what it lacked in sound it made up for in grandeur of size. It was a gargantuan monstrosity made up of ranks of pipes filling the walls of the sanctuary. It had its own hydraulic lifts and everything! It was as if someone had discovered a gigantic organ laying in a field and said, "Hey, let's build a church around that!"

I knew that none of my nightclub clothes would work in this big church with the big organ, so I had to purchase my first suit. It's hard to find a suit for a man with my measurements, and they don't come cheaply. I couldn't pick up my size at a secondhand store, and I needed a little more customization than can normally be purchased on a first paycheck budget. I eventually found a blue, crushed-velvet beauty, and I wore it every Sunday because it was the only suit I owned.

I was now a certified, suit-owning, paycheck-earning master worship leader responsible for an eclectic group of musicians whose organ hardware far surpassed anyone's musical aptitude. The diverse worship team included an absolutely amazing 85-year-old lady playing the blessed organ, who happened to be the best musician of the bunch, but was trapped in a 1950 time warp. Another equally proficient senior lady plucked away at the baby grand piano. We had a bass player who always roamed the stage aimlessly in search of the right listening position in order to hear himself louder through the house system, even though he had his own amp. And to top off the group, we had a guitarist who looked like he had just stepped out of the band Lover Boy—cut-off sleeves, headband, and all.

So week after week, I'd get up on the stage with the hydraulics in front of a band of musicians who weren't complementing each other, and somehow I had to lead the people into a place of worshiping God. Sometimes we had more success than others. Some people loved my changes and some people hated them.

Each Monday in staff meetings we were handed blue comment cards that were collected from the congregants. Some of the comments were constructive and useful, but I eventually learned to ignore most of what they said. "Why don't we have more drums?" "I want less drums!" "I really like when we sing hymns." "Hymns are outdated and I wish we wouldn't sing them." "Steve's suit is too tight. He looks like a sausage." Yes, really. Blue comment cards. Bad idea.

GROWING PAINS

The worship leading position was a challenge, and the stretching it caused ached at times. But the resulting growth was undeniable. In the middle of all the apparent chaos, God was breathing the Spirit of revival on this church. It was an absolutely sovereign work, because nothing we could have done could have generated such a sweet, healing presence in our midst. I was beginning to feel free again. Free to be led by the Spirit and enraptured by His presence. Free to love and be loved. Free to see God as He is and worship Him for that. I recaptured that freedom I had experienced as a child, only this time the freedom came with an awareness of the bondage from which I had been freed.

I ended up serving at that church for five years, and I experienced tremendous growth there. The growth wasn't all from positive experiences: I learned plenty about what I don't like about church politics. In fact there are a lot of similarities between church folk and some of the people who attend the clubs. You have the happy guys who loves everyone and make sure you know it. There's the grumpy guy who hates everything you do and can't wait for you to "take a break." Then there's the person who tragedy follows week after week and can never seem to get out of the rut.

Like my mom used to say, "God put me in grace boot camp for grace training."

But I also learned freedom again. I learned joy. I learned fulfillment in the presence of God. Through the process, God shaped me and molded me. Even though there were situations I didn't enjoy, I realize now the process developed me into the person God destined me to become. I also found a deep respect for pastors who have to deal constantly with issues week after week. God bless you!

Looking back on those years, I didn't realize what God was doing when He was doing it. At times I still felt lost and I yearned for understanding. But I knew I was in God's care, and I knew He had my back. He had a plan for my life, and He was going to see me through to that destiny.

My worship grew as my understanding of God grew. Now I could sing, "God, You are the Redeemer" and it meant something because I had been redeemed. I could sing, "You are my Fortress and my Healer" because He was, and is, the refuge from the chaos I had placed myself in. He healed my self-inflicted wounds caused by the years of running from Him. Suddenly, like David, I was creating my own psalms exalting God because I had personally experienced the God who rescued me.

My testimony became my song. My song became my worship. My worship led others into God's presence. In God's presence, they were also healed. That's what Revelation 19:10 means when it states, "the testimony of Jesus is the spirit of prophecy." My songs extolling the wonders of a gracious God were my testimony of Jesus' love for me. As I sing that testimony, it breaks open the prophetic potential for others to experience God in the same ways I have. God's gift to me became the breakthrough for others. The sung testimony releases Heaven on earth for those who hear.

During our lives we all struggle. In fact, we are warned of difficulties. Jesus told us in John 16:33, "In the world you will have tribulation; but be of good cheer, I have overcome the world." Our joy doesn't come from knowing that life will always be easy. Our joy comes in knowing the One who has overcome every obstacle. Our joy comes in our nearness to Him who loves us in, and around, and through the hard times.

David was a psalmist who also knew hard times. During a terrible time when he spent years fleeing for his life from Saul who was determined to end his life, he wrote these words: "Many are the afflictions of the righteous, but the Lord delivers him out of them all" (Psalm 34:19). Our goal in life isn't to accept affliction, but rather to seek the Deliverer who loves to rescue us. The One who loves us and revives us and uplifts us. When we have Him, we can have joy in any circumstance. As we yield to His direction, any detour can be used by Him to bring us back into our destiny.

He has wonderful plans for your life! He promises you a future and a hope (see Jeremiah 29:11). You were formed in the glory and He will see you through to the glory again. Your destiny was formed in His heart, and His sovereign hand will guide you there.

BACK ON TRACK

No amount of running away could ever erase God's destiny on my life. He was so good and so gracious to send divine encounters to turn me back toward the destiny-track of my life. He sent the lady on the train, Timothy and Deborah. He sent countless other people, circumstances, and places across my path at just the right moments to realign me with His glory. That's how much He loves me—and that's how much He loves you, too!

So much has happened since those early days in that large Portland church. About twelve years ago while we were still at that church, God led Lisa and me to develop a vision statement for our lives. The whole church engaged in the process to hear God's heart for our destiny as a church and then make a vision statement for where we had been and where we are going. But Lisa and I also wrote one for ourselves, and God helped us see where He was taking us. Now, years later, we are finally beginning to see some of those things come to pass.

We've created The Fourth Door Worship Arts Healing Center. We purchased two commercial units—one for our office and one for meetings and art classes. Fourth Door is a place dedicated to the presence of God demonstrated through the arts, worship, and healing. Our goal is to create a greenhouse atmosphere where we cultivate the very presence of God. We host art classes in which people can explore God's heart through all the arts.

We have worship services in which we simply spend time adoring God and inviting His presence to come and heal those who are ill. We truly believe in the laying on of hands for healing, but the premise of The Fourth Door Worship Arts Healing Center is different from that. We invite people to come and simply soak in the presence of God as we worship and cultivate the arts. God Himself lays His hands on them, and we have experienced some amazing miracles. There have been many testimonies of people receiving physical healing simply by being in God's presence. When God heals sovereignly, no one can claim the glory. All glory goes solely to the Healer.

Our goal is simply to create an atmosphere of worship in which the presence of God finds a home, then through the miracles, signs and wonders follow His presence. They happen as a side effect of pursuing God's presence. It's a refreshing place for those who are suffering under sickness and hardship to come, walk in the room, feel safe and loved, and not have to do anything. They just come into His presence and let His presence heal them. Sometimes the room is packed with people, and sometimes there are only one or two, but it doesn't matter because we aren't doing it for people. We are doing it for God. We are making a place for His presence to abide in our worship.

ADDICTED TO GOD'S PRESENCE

That is one key I have learned through this process. I've been on stages with thousands of people lifting their voices up to God. But I've also seen His glory come when it's just me, my piano, and Him. There's an exhilaration that comes with crowds of 7,000. It's a dream, really. But I've felt God's presence just as strongly with one or two as I have with multitudes. It doesn't matter to me. What matters is that I touch Him. That I lift Him up. That He is exalted in my praises.

And the amazing thing is that He also touches me when His presence comes. There is a divine exchange that happens in worship. It seems the more we bless Him, the more we get blessed—we certainly come out on the right end of that deal. How amazing is that!

I'm addicted. Addicted to God's presence. It's the place I'm always yearning to be. The secret place. It's the place I go back to and the place that keeps me going. It's the place where I receive the overflow. The overflow is what empowers me to keep going forward in His call and destiny for me. It's the overflow that brings the freedom. Freedom to love God. Freedom to be loved by Him. Freedom to follow Him with everything I have.

CHAPTER 2

THE SOUNDS OF HEAVEN

God loves sound. We can see magnificent and diverse examples of sound throughout the biblical narrative. The very first action recorded in the Bible was God producing sound. He *spoke* the words, "Let there be light," and there was light. God's voice was the progenitor of all creation. In Revelation 14:2, John describes God's voice as the sound of "many waters." Yet to Elisha it came as a "still, small voice" (1 Kings 19:12). Every sound finds its source in God.

However, God is not the only one who makes the sounds. All of Heaven is full of the music of praise. I call it the celestial symphony. John's vision of Heaven in Revelation 4 included four living creatures who perpetually proclaim, "Holy, holy, holy, Lord God Almighty, who was and is and is to come!" The throne room depicted in Isaiah's heavenly vision is similarly described with six-winged seraphim declaring to one another, "Holy, holy, holy is the Lord of hosts; the whole earth is full of His glory!" The power of their sound was so great that the throne room's doorposts were shaken by their praise (Isaiah 6:3-4).

Ezekiel's vision of Heaven included mighty creatures whose wings created a noise that was a "tumult like the noise of an army" (Ezekiel 1:24). All around us in the heavenly realm, angelic beings are singing God's praises. The sounds of angels and the sound of the movement of God's spirit compose a never-ending heavenly sound: Heaven's symphony. It moves and rolls and bellows and thunders. It never ceases to declare God's wonders.

God's heavenly creations aren't the only ones who craft the symphony of worship. The earthly creation sings God's praises as well. Isaiah 55:12 tells us that "the mountains and the hills shall break forth into singing before you, and all the trees of the field shall clap their hands." In Psalm 65:13, the pastures and the valleys "shout for joy, they also sing." First Chronicles 16:32-33 extols all of creation to worship: "Let the sea roar, and all its fullness; let the field rejoice, and all that is in it. Then the trees of the woods shall rejoice before the Lord."

All creation was designed for praise. It's in nature's nature to give God the glory due His name. They can't help it. They see His beauty and they awe. The problem with us as humans is that we have free will. We can choose to ignore the Beauty set before us. Romans 8:22 tells us that all of creation is groaning in longing for the day when we, the sons and daughters of God, will be revealed. They are waiting for us to join in the symphony of praise. Creation eagerly awaits our contribution, our harmony to be added to the symphony.

UNLIMITED WORSHIP

Worship cannot be stopped. Jesus told the Pharisees who were rebuking His disciples for worshiping Him that if they ever stopped, then the rocks would shout out their praise instead.

Sometimes, as worship leaders in churches, we mistakenly think that we have to bring something. We have to create something. We have to produce sounds and lyrics and spoken words to cause worship to happen. We believe that because we don't see people worshiping, we must create worship and lead people to that place we create. That is a very humanistic and works-centered view of worship. We start thinking that when our eyesight has become narrowed. Our senses have become limited to our five physical senses, and our faith in God's provision of worship has faltered.

Worship can never be stopped, even if we tried. Even if it weren't for the heavenly angels, the living creatures, the rocks, hills, fields, and trees, God is triune; He is Father, Son, and Holy Spirit. Even if there were no creation, the Trinity would exist in eternal adoration of each other. They can't stop loving on each other. Out of the overflow of that love came a creation that echoed Their cry.

So we don't bring worship. We don't do anything to create or cause it. No amount of prayer, musicianship, or leading can start worship. We simply join it. It's the realm that's already established by the ancient chorus. We join what all of creation, seen and unseen, is already doing perpetually. Joining is so much simpler than creating. We often strive too hard in worship, simply because we're not aware of Heaven's symphony, the atmosphere of Heaven. Our praise is just one instrument, one counterpoint, to a grand opus of song being raised continually to God. But ours is a very significant contribution. Ours is the sound of God's sons and daughters, the only ones created in His image. As His image-bearers, we are most fit, above all of natural creation, to praise.

Just because Heaven's symphony is constantly swirling around us doesn't always mean that we are cognizant of it. Sometimes God graces us with the ability to hear it, but often we must simply access it by faith. Like the wind, which is always present but we only tend to notice it when it shifts or intensifies, Heaven's symphony is often unnoticed until God's presence stirs it to our awareness.

When I worship, I try to be aware of the symphony encompassing me. God has had me on a journey to learn more about the constant worship around us, and I am awed at the things I have seen and heard.

Remember the mammoth organ church? God had a mark on that church. There was a remnant there who desired to see a move of God. Shortly after I accepted the worship-leading position there, they sent a few of us to a Kent Henry conference. Kent Henry is a worship leader and prophetic minister. He's a good friend of mine now, but at that time I had never actually attended a worship conference, so it was a new environment for me.

During one of the sessions, I was watching Kent play the piano when, suddenly, I began to feel like I was going to die. I started having a vision—more like an out-of-body experience—of my head on Kent's body while he was playing the piano. I kept rubbing my eyes, and I really felt that something was direly wrong. I couldn't get the vision out of my mind, and I didn't know what to do. I supposed because I was at a worship conference, I should use my dislocated head to sing and worship God. As I worshiped, I felt golden threads encircle me. I felt as though I was surrounded by God and destiny all at the same time. As my head was on Kent's body at his piano leading worship, I could see what God had planned for me. That vision propelled me forward into that function of leading worship into new realms. It was one of those moments when my obedience put me right where I needed to be for God to launch me further into my destiny.

Not long after that conference, our church invited Kent to come one Sunday. As Kent led worship, the church exploded with God's presence. People were jumping over pews, waving flags through the aisles, and praying throughout and over the sanctuary. It was revival. Fifteen hundred people wrecked in the presence of God.

PROPHETIC WORDS

During that weekend, Kent spent some time praying over Lisa and me. He read our mail. Prophesied our destiny. The word God gave him changed our lives. Sometime later, Kent came to do a weeklong event, paying his own expenses just to come be with us. It was a week of basking in the Lord. Again, he prophesied over me. He kept prophesying about songs, songs to the nations, songs from Heaven, and the sound of songs coming from Heaven to earth through me.

Those prophetic words changed everything for me. They didn't just foretell what God was going to do through me, they hurled me into that function. From then after, songs started flowing out of me. I couldn't stop them. Sometimes two or three whole songs a day. There were so many songs that I decided to record my first live CD. That recording carried the spirit of revival on it, and it captured what God was doing in the church at that time.

During this time, several of the pastors visited Toronto and the renewal hit our church. Not everybody liked what we were doing though. One week the church was running 1,500 people. The next week 600 showed up. By the third week, only 300 people braved their way to church. The Spirit of God was falling and breathing the Spirit of revival into the church, but not everyone chose to take the journey with us. It was an amazing time, and I wouldn't change it for anything.

So in the midst of all this upheaval, we had three different services at the church—more like a smorgasbord of pick your favorite style. Sunday morning was high church for the people who wanted their "normal" church back so they didn't feel like they had been invaded by the shakers. On Sunday night we held renewal meetings that would often last until the early morning hours. On Wednesday evening, we would do nothing but worship.

On one of those Wednesday nights in 1999 after I had led worship, a man approached me. "Have you heard about what's going on in Kansas City?" he asked.

I didn't have a clue what he was referring to.

He continued, "They are starting a house of prayer that runs 24-7. Just like in Heaven. They lift up songs of worship 24-7, like in Heaven."

24-7? It seemed a little strange to me. *Just like Heaven.* I was intrigued, and it got me wondering, *What is Heaven like? What does worship sound like in Heaven? Can I actually hear those sounds and reproduce them here on earth?*

He interrupted my thoughts with, "I got you a ticket. We're going to fly to Kansas City to check this out." I was ecstatic.

During the whole flight I was anticipating what it might be like to be in a place that worships God 24-7 just like Heaven. We arrived at the International House of Prayer to find a little trailer with carpet that needed to be stretched, and I saw three people sitting in the room with laptops. At the front of the room stood three men playing acoustic guitar accompanied by one guy on a Djembe drum. There was also a man to the side screaming something I couldn't understand. The guitarists strummed G, G, G, G, C, C, C, G, G, G, G, G, C, C, C, C, G for two hours. The monotony was occasionally broken up by the screaming man or a singer offering simple oohs and ahhs and words I didn't understand.

This is just like Heaven? Two chords and three laptops is Heaven? This can't be a good thing. I'm educated! I'm a former raisin! Couldn't they at least throw in a D every once in a while?

That night as I slumbered on a lumpy hotel mattress, I awoke about 4:30 in the morning to the sound of G, G, G, G, C, C, C, G, G, G, G, G, C, C, C, C, G in my ears. Something in my heart clicked. I didn't know why, but I had the insatiable desire for more G and C! I walked down to the house of prayer in the dark, and my eyes and heart opened up to what was happening. It wasn't about G and C anymore. It was about what they were singing, songs of revelation. I heard what I had been deaf to the night before—they were singing the songs of Heaven, and I was in awe. I had to have that.

Then God spoke to my heart, "Steve, this is what I want you to do."

"G and C?"

"No, Steve. I want you to sing the songs of Heaven. I want you to release the sound of Heaven on earth."

Suddenly I wished I had my laptop! *I have to write this stuff down. No wonder these people have their computers. I should have clued in!*

The rest of my time there I spent in worship and also attending the Song of Solomon workshop. The revelation I received on the Bride of Christ rocked me, and I even went out and bought a wedding dress—ha ha! I was completely transformed; wrecked and ruined for anything else but the heavenly hymns of revelation and the Song of Solomon.

OUR OWN HOUSE OF PRAYER

So I went back to the organ church and tell them we are going to start a 24-7 house of prayer and asked, "Who's in with me?" Well, three people were with me, so maybe not 24-7. So we started slowly with a few hours here and there. Eventually we transitioned to our own house of prayer—a little house sandwiched between two skyscrapers. Very rarely would we have a large number of participants. Ninety-nine percent of the time, it was just me, the singer, and the prayer leader. I would wonder why nobody wanted to pray. But I wasn't too bothered by it because I was caught up in the celestial symphony.

Usually I played the piano for a couple of hours as others soaked and devoted their worship to God. Then we would have a time of intercession. We would sing it and we would proclaim it. We'd worship with the songs of Revelation. Even as people walked by our windows, oblivious and uncaring toward the prayer and intercession going on, I was enraptured in the heavenly sounds.

It's in those moments when it's just you and nobody else—just you and God—when you begin to sow into your soul. You sow into His presence. You sow into the glory. You are sowing into yourself at that point, declaring that you are going to worship God regardless what anybody else does.

A lovely lady named Rainee would regularly come to the house of prayer. She always came after the first two hours for the second two hours of intercession. I anticipated her arrival. Rainee was blind, and she toted a braille Bible and sat at a big table we would set up just for her. She would immerse herself in worship, singing, "Jesus, You're so beautiful. Jesus, You are lovely." She'd place her fingers on the lines of raised letters in her Bible and begin singing the words she read. I envied her ability to *touch* God's *words*. I would often weep over the beauty stirred by this woman's devotion.

"SIT UP AND WORSHIP ME."

One evening, I was exhausted. About three hours into prayer, my hands had sunk into the keyboard, and I could hardly stay awake. My elbows were resting on my knees, propping up my body so I could continue to play. Unexpectedly, I felt two hands lift me from underneath my armpits and sit me straight up in my chair. "Sit up, and worship me," I heard God say in my spirit.

A new realm opened up for me in the Spirit at that moment. I looked at my hands playing the keyboard, and I could suddenly hear in them something I had never heard before though the notes were the same. I could hear ladies singing "worthy" while I played with my right hand and men singing "worthy" as I played with my left. Where was the sound coming from? It wasn't coming from our singer, because she was singing something else entirely. But I could hear them—voices joining with my hands. I couldn't tell if I was playing what they were singing or they were singing what I was playing.

I call it the simultaneous transcription of Heaven. The sounds of Heaven became translated into an earthly sound I could hear. As I watched my hands, they would join in with Heaven's sound that already existed in another dimension. I realized I couldn't even play the things my hands were doing. Then I started hearing a high soprano voice sustained over the moving parts. I knew the voice wasn't from anyone in our room, and yet I could hear it in the room just like I heard Rainee's worship.

After that night, I launched on a quest to recapture that sound. Find it again, relive it, and release it into the atmosphere. I would sit at my piano day after day yearning to hear it again. I've never heard it quite the same as I heard it that night, but I've heard variations and colors and shadows of it. I'm still on the quest; once I had tasted that celestial worship, nothing else compared. Nothing compares to the experience of God's presence in such a tangible way. I also love sharing the testimony of that encounter, not just because it released something in me, but because the testimony releases the prophetic realm of possibility over other worshipers.

That encounter also shaped my music. My whole paradigm shifted for where I thought I was going musically. My entire style of worship transformed. I started releasing a new sound quilted together from older parts. I found myself incorporating classical musical theory with the groove of jazz riffs. The two morphed into a new sound, and the transformation mirrored the shaping of my character that was happening simultaneously.

THE DREAM

During this time when my musical craftsmanship was developing, I had one of the most significant instances of guidance from the Holy Spirit I have ever experienced. It was deposited in my life in the form of a vivid dream. As time has gone by, the dream has become even more important to me than when I first had it because we've walked out the steps of the dream.

I dreamed Lisa and I were on our way to go camping in the woods. We turned on the radio and heard a report of a bear roaming the woods and mauling people. The radio announcement warned to watch for a dog, because a dog always preceded the bear. If you saw the dog, the bear was nearby. As I listened to this report, I rolled down the car windows. In the distance, I could hear the sound of the bear in the woods. We found a cabin and sought refuge there. Once inside, we saw the cabin was filled with people from our church in Portland, including many recognizable and prominent people. Then I realized the cabin was made out of dangerously thin balsa wood. I knew the balsa wood would never withstand a bear attack. I was afraid for our friends because I knew they wouldn't survive under the pressure or power of the bear. I told Lisa we had to get out of there, so we escaped through the back door.

As we walked down a hill, I could still hear the bear growling in the distance. We eventually reached a street corner with a bus stop. As we approached, we noticed three figures dressed in black trench coats, like in *The Matrix*. They were getting on the bus and they said to us, "Don't worry about the bear. Just go back. Go back."

As I turned, I could see a dog approaching us. I moved my arms out, and they morphed into weapons. One arm was a crossbow and one was a spiked ball and chain. I was ready to take the dog on, but then I got a better look at the dog. It was pathetic. It looked malnourished and weak. Despite the dog's frailty, I was aware that it was the antecedent of the bear. So I urged Lisa for us to go quickly.

We ran down the street and found a building with a glass door. It was surrounded with one-way glass, and I was relieved that this shelter was much stronger than the balsa wood cabin we had been in previously. At least we would be able to see out and the bear couldn't see in. There was also a long bar countertop, like you would find in a Waffle House restaurant. So we hid under the counter, and we knew we were safe from the bear's detection.

As we were hiding in the glass house, the bear strolled down the street, trying to hunt us down. But it walked right past us because it couldn't see through the glass. However, I still didn't feel that we were safe. If the bear somehow discovered we were in there, he could break through the glass. So we decided to move on before the bear noticed our presence.

We came upon a castle door constructed from thick wood and decorated with weighty iron hinges and a bold knocker. *This is good,* I thought. It offered much more protection than balsa wood or glass. As I opened the door, I realized the interior didn't match the formidable exterior. It looked like we stepped inside a smoky 1960s Italian restaurant. Burgundy, puffy booths with checkerboard tablecloths filled the room, and a band played in the back. Maybe it wasn't as safe as we thought. So we decided to shut the castle door and walk farther.

"I know a place we can go," I said in the dream. I led the way to a marina. As we walked along the marina, I saw a four-story tall tower. It was guarded by two sentries like the ones who guard Windsor Castle in England. A revolving door served as the only entrance to the building. An elevator led to the fourth floor. I thought this location was perfect. There was no way the bear could get past the guards. If it managed to get past the guards, it would find itself going in circles and circles in the revolving door. There was no way the bear could know how to operate an elevator. I knew we were safe at last.

ARCADIA

After I had the dream, I was trying to make sense of it all, and I recounted it to my mom. I was puzzled by the marina, because in the dream I had known the place. She reminded me of a marina we had once visited called Arcadia. I researched the word "arcadia" and discovered that it means a rural pasture, a peacefully valley, a place of peace. I realized then that the Lord was saying He would lead us to new places. I was comforted by the knowledge that His peace, His arcadia would be with us.

So on Christmas Day, we relocated from Portland, Oregon, our home for more than 40 years. We headed to a new position I had been offered in western Kentucky, and we never turned back. We had rented a house sight unseen, and when we arrived there, our real estate agent warned us that the house was a little unusual. It had a room made completely of one-way glass and had a countertop bar like a Waffle House. It had commercial doors and fixed windows with one-way glass, and there was no drywall in the room. The walls were made from beveled glass mirrors. He was afraid we would hate the location, but we were thrilled. It was identical to the building in my dream. God was confirming to us that we were exactly on track. We were precisely where He wanted us to be.

Just because we were where God wanted us didn't mean we felt at home, yet. Here I was, a lifelong resident of Portland—the greenest, tree-huggingest, most liberal state in the union—stuck in the middle of a cornfield in Kentucky.

I'm pretty sure they spoke English there, but Lisa and I often had to translate for each other, and we were often left befuddled for the first several months till we started to pick up some of the dialect.

We loved the church there. It was what I call a river church. It was in a state of revival, and the Spirit of God would move so strongly there. My favorite feature of this church was my office, a tiny eight-by-eight room with blue stained glass. When the sun would shine through the windows, the whole room would light up in marvelous hues of blue. I called it my blue chamber. I would lock myself in the blue chamber and play for hours, just me and Jesus.

I began writing songs of intimacy, songs of the bride. I was hearing sounds that I attempted to capture, and I was on a quest to mimic the swooshes and wisps and bellows. I had to find a way to make those sounds, so I purchased a bunch of keyboards. I brought them all up on the platform with me in an attempt to formulate the orchestra that would release the sound of Heaven. I worshiped for months with those keyboards trying to release the celestial sounds.

One day as I was worshiping in the blue room, a five-year-old girl came in. "I'm a daddy's girl," she said. Her name was Rachel, and I fell in love with her. Rachel had a brain tumor, and she had survived having shunts placed in her head and multiple surgeries. But despite all the trauma she had been through and the tumor still threatening her fragile brain, Rachel had the sweetest disposition and a heart overflowing with love.

The Lord put me on assignment to sing and play and pray over Rachel. It was an assignment I treasured. Twice a week, we would go to her house to the back bedroom that housed a little Spinet piano. Rachel's mom, Lisa, and I would spend hours worshiping God and singing from the Psalms. We were creating an atmosphere for healing to come. We made many declarations of faith in that little room as we worshiped God. We truly believed that God was doing a miracle in Rachel's brain, and she experienced several significant breakthroughs in the battle with the cancer. We experienced many victories, and we noticed that she especially enjoyed when we would worship with joy. She'd bound off the bed and start dancing around.

An Atmosphere for Healing

It was in that little room with Rachel that I learned about creating an atmosphere for healing and being able to sing the Psalms. We declared God's heart for healing over Rachel through song. It was a time of preparation for what lay ahead for us. It was at that Spinet piano that the Lord taught me about the psalmist's anointing. The "psalmist anointing" creates an atmosphere for God's presence to rest on. It fosters an environment fertile for healing to be released.

The Lord would place a psalm on my heart, and I would just sing from the psalm. During that time, I wrote several hundred songs as I spent time with the Lord interceding for this little girl.

Rachel eventually passed away. We really struggled. We asked all the why questions. We had sown so much in prayer. We had sown so much in worship. We had sown so much in our tears. Now she's gone. But I had to remind my soul that God's ways are higher. God had a plan. All that time spent in that little room with the little piano were recorded in Heaven. We had also recorded much of it down here to leave with her mom to comfort her.

My years in Kentucky were a significant time that taught me that we didn't need a big crowd. We never need large numbers to produce substantial results. After all, we are joining in a heavenly chorus that began ages ago, and it resounds in the atmosphere as all of the angels and creation join in. Only faith the size of a mustard seed is required to open the doors of Heaven and release the healing sounds.

CHAPTER 3

THE SOUNDS
OF EARTH

We spent a few years in Kentucky, and God used that time to shape us and refine our calling. God met me and molded me in the blue chamber and Rachel's house. I learned more in those short years about worship, healing, and God's sound than in any other time of my life.

Then God called us to a church in Englewood, Florida. They had a strong focus on healing, and that had been exactly what God had been stirring in my heart. We had wonderful Sunday night services that centered on healing and worship. We would flow in and out—worship and healing then healing and worship—and it was absolutely beautiful. The pastor was a warm, gentle man who would worship for hours by simply sitting in the service and loving on Jesus. He wasn't demonstrative at all, never would raise his voice, just a gentle lover of God, and I really came to love that man.

One day, the youth pastor approached me with a mischievous smile. "Hey Steve, do you want to see a video of Pastor? It's from when he went to Brazil with Randy Clark."

"Sure," I said, not sure what about a missions video could be so amusing. Then as I watched, I saw our put-together, gentle pastor writhing on the ground seemingly in pain, shouting out "RAAAHHH" and "AAAGH."

"Is that our pastor?" I asked in unbelief.

"Yes, that's Pastor. This is what happened when he went on a trip to Brazil with Randy Clark. We are going to a Randy Clark conference next week."

"We? You mean me too?"

"Yes. We! We are going to a Randy Clark conference next week."

I looked again at the video of Pastor contorting and shouting and wondered just what I was in for.

Randy is a man who walks in a lot of power and sees a lot of healing, but he is very passionate about releasing that same anointing over others. At nearly every conference, he shares a couple of messages that are dear to his heart. One is "God Can Use Little Ole Me,"[1] meaning the Holy Spirit desires to move through and with each of us, regardless how insignificant we think we are in the kingdom of God. The second message he shares often is on impartation of spiritual gifts.

On this night, Randy was sharing the impartation message, and he started praying impartation for people. I had decided to hang out in the back row, out of the range of potential pain, writhing, and shouting. Randy stated, "Sometimes the Lord will come on you so powerfully that you feel like you are going to die." *Die? I don't want to be part of that!*

He continued, "You feel like you're going to die, like you plugged yourself into 220." *But I don't want to feel like I'm going to die! How can that be a good thing?*

"Sometimes the weight feels so heavy that it's like a dentist's apron upon your chest. If you feel that weightiness now, don't get up." I didn't.

I was glad I was safely secluded in the back row, because I really didn't want to die. Just to be sure, I tucked myself behind the pole you can find at the back of most sanctuaries, far out of Randy's line of sight.

"I'm not going to touch anybody at all." *Oh, thank God!* "But when I see the Lord moving on you, I'm going to bless what He's doing in Jesus' name." *Okay. I can handle that. I'll just sit here on the back row behind the pole and see what happens.*

"Worship leader from Englewood!" *What? Did Randy just call out a worship leader from Englewood? Wait! I'm a worship leader from Englewood!* "Worship leader from Englewood, God is going to open up more realms of Heaven to you like you've never heard before. What you've heard in the past is nothing compared to what He's going to give to you right now in Jesus' name. I bless what You're doing, Father."

"I'M GOING TO DIE!"

It was as if a fist struck me in the chest when Randy spoke those words. They stunned me, and the power they imparted knocked me back. Then the next thing I experienced was a sound. It was like a fax machine sound. Then all these notes started coming in from the all sides. I was caught up in this sound, and my head and body followed the notes up and down as I heard them swirl past me. Up and down and up and down for forty-five minutes. The weight and power they carried was so strong. I starting thinking to myself, *I'm going to die! I really think I'm going to die!*

Suddenly the fax sound stopped, and I was knocked off my feet. I bounced three times and no one even tried to catch me. Then I was writhing and contorting! *I'm going to die!* As I became acutely aware of a pain in my side from the fall, I realized that I must still be alive—but barely. I was on the floor, flat on my back, unable to comprehend all that was happening to me.

My eyes were closed, and I was looking into the back of my eyelids. As I looked, I saw a mist. I tried to look deeper, though I realized how odd it was that I was looking deeper into my own eyelids. Nearby, I heard a lady with a crowd of people, and they were all crying in tongues. That sound intensified the vision I was having of the mist. Out from the mystery of the sound and the mist, I could feel the Lord grab me, pull me upward, and drop me into a village in Africa. The sound of the lady praying had caused it; I could tell because her tongue sounded like an African language, and it had somehow formed a portal for me to be transported to Africa in this vision.

I started walking down a street in Africa. A blue bike leaned against a post to my right. A child darted across the road. Dirt gutters lined the streets. The sounds of Africa—drums and laughter and dance—flooded my awareness. I was simultaneously present in an African village and also on a floor in the United States cognizant of the vision. I was aware both of the lady praying in tongues near me and children playing in the street in Africa.

As I was experiencing this vision, someone turned on a large fan near the back of the sanctuary, not far from where I was laying. The whoosh of the fan pulled me into its sound. I was sucked into a plane by the fan's whirl, and I was flying over a river in Africa. I could tell I was still in Africa because I could see giraffes, zebras, and elephants roaming the savannah below me. Hippos dotted a lake as we flew over it and away from Africa. Then I was dropped to another place, and a new vision opened up to me.

I saw the Lord and a map of the world. Then God reached down and grabbed Mexico and pulled all of North America off the map. He took the peninsula of Florida and dipped it into a vat of oil three times. Dip, dip, dip. As oil was dripping down Florida, He said, "That's the wick." A glow lit up the coastline of the gulf and swirled up the eastern seaboard. Then winds blew in from the west and ignited the glow into a flame. A fire swept up the East Coast.

At some point Randy became aware that something was happening with me. I don't know at what point I came to his attention because I was lost in the visions. But I found myself on the stage in front of 1,200 people, and Randy was having fun with me. "So Steve, tell us what you see."

"I…see…whoosh! And hrummmph! Then a shhhooom! Blooowww!" I'm pretty sure I didn't make any sense, but I could hear everything God was doing, and it was amazing.

To this day, I'm not sure exactly what God was doing in the visions, but I know I was changed instantaneously. If I had met someone at the beginning of the meeting, I'm pretty sure they wouldn't have been able to recognize me as the same person by the end of the meeting. I had received a download from God, and just as Randy had prophesied, a new realm of sounds opened up over my life. A level of fluidity that I hadn't experienced came effortlessly through my music and worship leading. The anointing I experienced at the conference remained with me, and I felt as if I was living in a new realm of sounds and visions all the time.

REVELATION 4

One afternoon as I was studying in my bedroom, God started a conversation with me.

"Steve, I want to do a project with you."

"That sounds like fun, God. What kind of project?"

"I want to you to open your Bible to Revelation 4."

"Revelation 4?" I remembered Revelation 4. That's John's vision of the throne room in Heaven in which the elders and the living creatures cry out "Holy" and throw their crowns down before the throne in eternal worship. I felt like a grenade had been thrown into my spirit and at any second it was going to explode.

"Yes, I want you to read it." I had read it a thousand times and knew what to expect, so I was excited to read it again with Him.

I started reading it to Him.

> "After these things I looked, and behold, a door standing open in heaven. And the first voice I heard was like a trumpet speaking with me, saying, 'Come up here, and I will show you things which must take place after this.' Immediately I was in the Spirit; and behold, a throne set in heaven, and One sat on the throne. And He who sat there was like a jasper and a sardius stone in appearance; and there was a rainbow around the throne, in appearance like an emerald."

God interrupted me. "No. You're not getting it. Read it again."

So I read it again.

"You're still not getting it. I want you to underline every word that has a sound in this passage and read it again."

I did what He said, but I still knew I was missing something. I needed to approach this differently. I had to get away from the pen and paper and written words. I thought about a keyboard I had recently bought, and I realized that God wanted me to create something with Him. I didn't really know where to start, so I figured I'd start at square one. The keyboard has the ability for me to write my own patches from scratch, so I started taking the factory patches and tweaking them. I was trying to emulate the sounds I could hear in my head as I visualized the scene from Revelation 4.

The sounds I was creating were amazing and baffling. "Lord, what are these sounds? They don't sound like anything I've typically heard in worship. How can I ever use these patches in worship?"

"Just trust Me."

"Okay, I'll trust You." So I continued crafting new patches I had never heard before and weaving them together into a tapestry of sound. I still wasn't sure what they all meant. "What's this all about, God?"

"I want to put these sounds to a track. I want you to bring Revelation 4 to life."

So what does Revelation 4 sound like? I didn't know what the finished sound would be like, but from the passage, I could pinpoint certain components. So I started throwing in lightning and thunder, voices, and the sound of many waters. I became a mad scientist at my keyboard. Throw in a dash of rumble and a hint of a clank! My office at church became the boiling pot in which I was simmering in a concoction of heavenly sound.

What does many waters sound like, I asked myself. So I started constructing it one water at a time. A babbling brook. A flashing waterfall. A gentle rain. A swelling ocean. A terrifying storm. I had all these waters, but how would they ever work together? It would be overwhelming! So I constructed it one component at a time. Tweak some EQ here. Change frequencies there. Remove treble here. Boost bass there. I adjusted volumes, regulated pitches, and synchronized sounds until it wasn't so overwhelming and it sounded right. It sounded like ultra sound. Like we were birthing something together. It was a mystery and a delight. Quite a project that I will never forget.

NATURE'S CHOIR

On a different occasion, I was listening to another track I had been working on when God spoke to me. "Steve, I want you to put the sound of the cricket in there."

"A cricket? Really?"

"Yes, Steve. A cricket. I want you to add the sound of the cricket in this track."

So where can I find a cricket? Google has crickets. Or my friend Don, the sound genius. I called Don and asked him to send me over some cricket sounds. I sampled the sound of the cricket. (Sampling allows you to take a sound, layer it, and play several layers at the same time.) I was having a blast at my sound equipment, sampling crickets. Adding in more crickets, changing their pitches, and speeding up and slowing down their sound. I was doing something I never would have imagined: I was playing crickets! Three crickets then four crickets. Soon I had a whole cricket choir.

"Steve," God interrupted my cricket choir rehearsal.

"Yes, God?"

"I want you to take it down a couple octaves." So I lowered the crickets a couple octaves. I was stunned as I realized the sound resembled a chorus of birds at that lower pitch. Now I was playing bird choruses!

"Take it down a little farther, Steve." Then the cricket chorus has transformed into the low hoot of an owl.

"Keep taking it down. Down. All the way down there." I did, and wow! It was like the low, rumbling, of a whale's song.

"See, Steve? They are all singing the same song. All creation sings the same song; they just sing it at different frequencies."

Then I got it! From the greatest to the least, all of creation is in Heaven's symphony of worship unto the Lord. Every spectrum of sound generated by all the diversities represented in creation all sing the same chorus of praise to the Lord. All of what can be heard with our ears and that which can't, it all resolves to the same song. It all goes back to adoration of the Creator.

I started freaking out. I'm a master composer in an orchestra of creation. Throw in the owls here, and counter with the whales! Crickets harmonizing to the melody of the birds!

After a few hours confined in my eight-by-eight room with my massive speakers and all creation swirling around me, I was getting a little frazzled. I'm pretty sure that between my mad-scientist crafting and the sound blasting from the speakers, my hair had spiked out in every direction. I had to get out of there to get some quiet.

I strolled down to my favorite location in Florida, out on the bay. It was a quiet place where I could look out into the ocean, and the dolphins would sometimes meander by in the beautiful turquoise water. *At last,* I thought to myself, *some peace and quiet. No more sounds for a while.*

Just as I'm relaxing into the joy of the silence, a tiny flash of light hit my eye. The gentle waves would roll. As they did, the sunlight would catch them for an instant, reflecting the light. I was mesmerized by the sight of a mirage of flashes of light when I heard it—ting! Then again. Ting! Ting! Ting! It sounded like a triangle. With every rustle of wind lifting the waves came a flash of light accompanied by a ting. Every reflection of light was singing, "Ting!"

Oh no! I came here for some quiet, and now I can't escape it. It's not just the crickets. It's the waves, too.

So I looked away from the waves and my eyes fell on a perfectly formed yellow dandelion. The wind bristled against it and I hear "huuussshhh." I'm staring at the singing dandelion when my thoughts are interrupted by a "whhhooommm." *What was that?* I looked up and saw the leaves of a palm tree rubbing up against each other in the breeze. Ting! Hush! Whoom!

77

Everywhere around me there was sound!

"Do you see, Steve?" I hear God ask. "Do you hear it? All creation is praising Me."

I had always known it. I had even taught on it. I had heard glimpses of it. But now I was immersed in the sound of the celestial symphony. I couldn't escape it. Everywhere, all of creation was lifting up their praise to God. It was an unstoppable force, and its immensity overwhelmed me. Music, sounds, and whooshes raised in a cacophony of worship to our God. The sounds had always been there, but I had taken them for granted. I hadn't appreciated the reverential devotion of all of creation to its Creator.

EVERY CORNER OF CREATION

A little while later, I visited Alaska for the first time. Alaska's landscape is riddled with enormous mountains that stretch as far as the eye can see. I grew up in Oregon with its single mountains, so I was taken aback by the plethora of so many mountains in Alaska spanning out in every direction. I could hear the sound there, too. It was beautifully unique from the sounds I heard in the Florida bay. The bay had a tranquil beach sound, and Alaska had a majestic mountain sound. I could hear Alaska rumbling under the weight of those fortresses of might. The mountains sounded like the march of an army parading forward for their God with a rumble of praise.

Each region has its own worship. Every location has its own sound. Florida has a sound, and Africa has a sound, and Alaska has a sound. Not only does the unique creation in each region raise its own symphony, but the people of that region echo the glories of what God has done there. The people of the Middle East sound different from the praises of the people in Western Europe. We all have a sound to contribute to bring glory to God in our regions. Our mountains, oceans, trees, and soil all sing out before us, and we join their chorus with our own sound.

We are all part of something much larger than ourselves. We are never alone in our worship. Even if we are the only person in the room, the ground itself shouts forth God's praises. It's not just us. There is something much greater than ourselves to which we are ascribing all our affection. We are pointing our worship to Him and we are joining in with an ancient, rumbling, bubbling sound that has been resonating for ages.

As God continued to speak to me about the heavenly symphony, I had a conversation about it with a man from New England. I was explaining how I can hear creation.

"Really?" he asked with intrigue.

"Yeah, I do. Well, not always. But yes, I can hear creation. It's kind of this realm that sometimes opens up to me."

"Wow! I want to hear creation," he proclaimed. "Could you pray for me right now? Pray for me to hear creation."

I prayed and asked God to open up the sounds of creation to this man. Then I asked him what happened as I prayed, and he said, "I don't hear anything. What am I supposed to do?"

"I don't really know. It's just something that opened up for me."

"Well, I don't hear it," he mumbled as he walked off.

A half hour later I got a phone call. "Steve! I can hear it!"

"Hear what?"

"I can hear creation! It's everywhere. It's all around me. All of creation is praising God all around me!"

"That's amazing!"

"Now how do you turn it off?"

Good question. Sometimes I wonder the same thing. We can't turn it off, because creation will never stop its chorus of adoration to God. But often my awareness of the sound wanes. When it does turn off, I long to hear it again. I'm on a constant quest to hear the sound, emulate the sound, reproduce the sound, and lead others into the sound.

I wasn't always able to hear the sound, but I have learned that awareness of its presence prophetically opens it up for me. When we meditate on the truth that we are surrounded by a symphony of praise, and trust that it's there—especially in those moments when we don't really feel like worshiping—it becomes easier for us to hear it. Worship is so much easier to do when we step into something that's already happening.

JOINING THE PRAISE CHOIR

When we follow the symphony and join our voices to the sound, it's an invitation and an on-ramp for others to follow us. We follow Heaven and creation, and then others follow us. Our worship opens the door for others to enter into worship. Even the lost will follow us. I have been in meetings where people have walked into the room, drawn into the worship by the sounds of our praise. One time this happened with a construction worker who was working on a project outside the building. He stepped about two feet into the sanctuary before he fell to his knees, overwhelmed by the beauty of God. Our sounds join the heavenly sounds and they beckon the lost to come and adore.

The celestial symphony stirs our sounds, and our sounds stir the symphony. We hear and we join, and the joining produces and exponentially increases in praise.

I'm often asked how to go to new dimensions in worship. We go to new dimensions as we lose our minds. We need to literally lose our minds. We set aside the entanglements of trying to figure it out. We let our minds go and stop thinking about everything so hard. Stop thinking about our jobs and our families and our bills and our junk. Instead, let it all go and worship.

Worship at its best is worship at rest. We rest in the understanding that when we worship, we are doing what we were most created for. It's effortless because it's our purpose, created to be loved and to love. Worship was our greatest intention from the beginning when God birthed us in glory. When we return to that glory, it's a place of rest, not striving. We reach a new dimension as we let go of all the entanglements and return to what we were created for—to enjoy the worship of God.

There is so much joy in worship. When we are focused on the beauty and splendor of God, how can our emotions remain entangled in fear or anger or sadness? All that is left to feel is joy. It's a joy that comes through nearness to the One who loves us best and loves us most.

You can experience that joy when you're worshiping in a crowd of thousands or worshiping alone in your room with Jesus. If you are a musician, you can worship with your instruments, or if not, just worship with the caress of your words. You don't have to be a musician to love worship, you just have to open your mouth and tell Jesus how holy He is, how lovely He is. If you can't find your own words, go to Scripture and pick out a psalm. You can also remind yourself of the wonders He has done in your life, and recount those moments back to Him in song. Find your joy in placing all your attention on Him who created you in an environment of worship and for the purpose of worship. Tell Him how much you love Him in a verse of praise.

Then listen. As you sing your melody of worship, you'll hear His harmony singing along with you: "I love you, too."

ENDNOTE

1. Randy Clark, *God Can Use Little Ole Me* (Shippensburg, PA: Destiny Image Publishers, 1998).

CHAPTER 4

KEYS TO JOINING
THE SYMPHONY

I've been spoiled. I've been ruined by the presence of God. I've been wrecked by the taste of His beauty, and I can't go back to mediocrity. Yet at the same time, there's a tension. The heavenly symphony surrounds us, but it's not always easy to enter in. There are times when our lives, our minds, our emotions, and other distractions seem like enormous walls preventing us from going where we want to go, to that place of worship.

Despite how much we know we should worship, challenges arise that pull like tethers on us, trying to keep us from God's presence. We become entangled in ourselves or snared by the enemy. It's not always easy to be present in worship. There were times in Rachel's house when I wanted to worship, but the gravity and sorrow of her declining health were obstacles I had to overcome. There have been times when I've been in services for five or six hours, and the sheer exhaustion becomes a barrier to praise. These are not times for us to pull back. These are times when we use the weapons God gave us to come into that place of agreement with the Spirit.

I love reading and worshiping to the psalms, especially David's psalms. I love his heart: a warrior, worshiper's heart. As you read them, the anguish and despair over his dire situations flow out from the words. He laments over the frustrations in his life and the unjust, relentless pursuit of the enemy. But keep reading. In each of those psalms, he always brings his song back to a place of worship. He centers his mind and heart back on the goodness, sufficiency, and worthiness of God. He even admonishes the weak spots within himself: "Why so downcast, oh my soul? Put your hope in God" (Psalm 42:5, paraphrased).

David lived in the same tension I do. I can really relate to him. I have my good days and my bad days. I have my days of victory and my days when the questions and doubts overrun the joy. But I've learned from the psalms that we aren't without resources when we are at the end of ourselves. The moment we have nothing more to give is the best moment to pull out our arsenal of worship. That's when we use our weapons of worship to fight through the entangling distractions and into the presence of God. The Holy Spirit is our Helper who makes sure we get there.

THREE KEYS

There are three keys I've discovered that can always be depended upon to help us enter God's presence and join Heaven's symphony: *thanksgiving, praise, and worship.* When we use these keys as weapons, we can combat any obstacles that prevent us from accessing God's presence and giving Him the glory due His name. These keys can be used in your individual worship and also in the art of leading others into a place of worship and intimacy with Christ.

When we worship, God's glory is revealed. When God's glory is revealed, there is power released. The manifest power of God changes the whole atmosphere around you. It transforms you from the inside out. It's the thanksgiving, praise, and worship that are our arsenal to unlock the glory and open up the heavenly realms. Then all we have to do is just stand and bask in His glory.

I have many favorite psalms, but there are a handful that perfectly describe the tools for entering into worship. They have been my guides when worship becomes hard. They serve as a template for how we can use these three keys of thanksgiving, praise, and worship to enter into God's presence. As we use the keys, they access the heavenly realms in which God's manifest presence and glory come, and we are undone.

Thanksgiving

The first key in our arsenal is thanksgiving. There is immense power in our gratitude. Take a look at Psalm 30.

I will extol you, O Lord, for You have lifted me up, and have not let my foes rejoice over me. O Lord my God, I cried out to You and You healed me. O Lord, You brought my soul up from the grave... (Psalm 30:1-3).

You can see in this psalm that David is reminding himself of his reasons to worship. He is recalling the mighty things God has done on his behalf. David cried out to God and God healed him. He brought David's soul up from the grave.

I don't know what it feels like to be lifted up from a literal grave. I would imagine that would be radically life-transforming. But I have been in my own figurative graves. My pursuit of music, fame, and wealth in my early adult years felt like a grave. I was absolutely dead on the inside. Completely incapable of anything but feeling pain. I tried to stuff that grave with cool gigs, late nights, friends, and artful musicianship, but a grave is a grave no matter what you fill it with. When God grabbed my attention and snatched me from my self-destructive path, I could relate to David's thanksgiving: "You brought my soul up from the grave."

Each of us has had similar experiences. We were once lost but now we are found. We were in our own grave, and we cried out to God and He healed us.

There have probably been several times in your life you can recall as a time when God brought your soul up from the grave. It may have been a grave of physical sickness, depression, addiction, or regret. But God was faithful to draw you out of that pit and bring you back into His destiny-path for your life. He is so kind and so generous. Remembering those moments is a key to thanksgiving. If you don't remember, you are unable to give thanks. Remembering and thanksgiving are two sides of the same coin. So when you have trouble being thankful, flip the coin over and spend time remembering. Remember His goodness.

I love the stories in the Old Testament about the forefathers of our faith. Every time God encountered them or delivered them, they would erect a monument to what God had done in that place. When Jacob had the angelic encounter where the heavenly realm was opened to him and he saw angels ascending and descending on a ladder to Heaven, he took a stone and set it as a pillar and anointed it with oil. When the Angel of the Lord appeared to Gideon and called him out of obscurity to lead the Israelites in battle against the Midianites, Gideon stacked a pile of rocks as an altar and named it "The Lord is Peace." He did it so that he and others would remember what the Lord had done on their behalf by bringing peace to their land. These markers served as reminders to all future generations of God's mighty faithfulness. They are recorded in the Bible as reminders to us as well. Even if you are struggling in despair so deep that you can't remember the times God has rescued you, you can go to the Word of God and see His faithfulness throughout all of human history. Claim their victories as your own.

Psalm 30 continues, "So play music in Yahweh's honor, oh those He loves" (Psalm 30:4, paraphrased). That's us!

We are the ones He loves. We play music in His honor for no other reason than He loves us. I could just bask in that word all day long. We play and sing because He loves us. Amazing!

Then David returns to thanksgiving in verses 11-12: "You have turned my mourning into dancing. You have stripped off my sackcloth and clothed me in a garment of joy. So will my spirit sing to you and not be silent. Oh, Lord my God, I will give thanks to you forever" (Psalm 30:11-12, paraphrased). This passage is rich with meaning, but the phrase that most sticks out to me is "my spirit will sing to you and not be silent." We were not created for silence. God gave us voices to sing and hands to clap and feet to stomp for a reason: to make sounds of praise to God.

Psalm 115:17 tells us that "the dead go down into silence and neither do they praise the Lord" (paraphrased). Silence is reserved for those who are dead. But we have been plucked from the grave! So we sing, we dance, we shout, and we praise. While we are living, we must use our time on earth to praise. The enemy wants us to be quiet. He doesn't like it when we proclaim the works of the Lord, because he knows that when we do, his strongholds in our lives and on the earth are destroyed. Every word of praise that passes our lips loosens the chains in our lives and those around us.

It's hard to be silent when you are joyful. Have you ever had really good news, and it was impossible not to share it? That's what joy does. We encounter joy in our nearness to God. It's a joy that bubbles up and overflows everywhere and makes messy puddles all around us. I call it the bubble factor—the overabundant, uncontainable, flowing-all-around-you kind of joy. Joy shows up on your face. It's impossible to be in the bubble factor with a frown. Sometimes when joy seems elusive, just tell your face to partner with joy. Turn your frown upside down and remember why you have a reason to worship. Making the choice to remember God's mighty deeds is an act of worship. It's thanksgiving, and it unleashes praise.

Psalm 89:15 tells us, "Blessed are the people who know the joyful sound! They walk, O Lord, in the light of Your countenance." When we know, remember, and agree with the joyful sound, we become blessed. Joy causes us to walk in the light of His countenance. What is His countenance like? It's full of glory, loving-kindness, righteousness, mercy, holiness, and might. All those things are imparted to us when we release the joyful sound.

Thanksgiving is an entryway for us. It's the gateway into God's presence. Psalm 100:1 says we enter His gates with thanksgiving. I want to enter into His gates, and the key is thanksgiving. One of the Hebrew words used in that verse is *towdah*. It's a root word for "praise," and is translated as "giving praise to God, thanksgiving in psalms of liturgical worship, hymns of praise, a thank offering, and a thanksgiving choir procession line or company." Can you imagine a whole thanksgiving choir procession line? It reminds me of the shouts of thanksgiving that were raised when David brought the Ark of the Covenant into Jerusalem. First Chronicles 15 tells us that the elders, the captains, the singers, and the Levites all accompanied the Ark the whole journey to Jerusalem. They gave thanks with shouting, horns, trumpets, symbols, stringed instruments, and harps.

I was once part of a worship service that included a thanksgiving procession. We actually commissioned a man to build us an ark to the correct dimensions and specifications in the Bible. We carried the ark as part of a thanksgiving procession to usher in the presence of God. It was a prophetic act in which we were actually bringing God's presence with us upon our praises. The event was very anointed, and it was also a lot of fun!

There's something magical about thanksgiving. It's a double-sided blessing because not only does it unlock our hearts into a place of worship, it also moves God's heart as well. Our thanksgiving can actually stir God's compassion on us and move Him to show His power on our behalf. Thanksgiving is a key to opening up the realm of the miraculous. There are several biblical examples of this.

In Matthew 15, Jesus had been teaching for days, and a crowd of 4,000 men had gathered to hear Him, not counting all the women and children who also came to hear Jesus. It was the third day, and Jesus felt compassion for people because they had been with Him for three days with no food. Jesus called His disciples together to discuss the situation. Jesus didn't want to send them away without feeding them, because they would be weak along the lengthy journeys to walk home on foot. So He asked the disciples how much food they had available.

"We only have seven loaves of bread and a few fish," they said.

That was good enough for Jesus. He asked the crowd to have a seat. He took a moment to give thanks to God for the seven loaves of bread and the few fish. He commanded the disciples to start distributing the bread and fish, and a miracle occurred. The food multiplied hundreds of times over until there was enough to fill every person there.

Notice that when the meal consisted of only seven loaves and a few fish, Jesus gave thanks. Though it was vastly inadequate for the hunger before Him, Jesus gave thanks. He was grateful for the gift of food, even though it was merely a tiny fraction of what was needed.

This act of thanksgiving demonstrates two realities. First, when our need seems to greatly surpass our provision, we need to take a moment like Jesus did and give thanks. Give thanks for what you do have, even if it's not sufficient to meet your needs. There is power released in our thanksgiving, and it is a power to release God's resources into our circumstances. Jesus' act of thanksgiving for what God had already given precipitated the miracle of an overabundance to meet all the needs. Sometimes what's holding God back from releasing blessing into our lives is the fact that He has already blessed us in a measure, and we fail to acknowledge it. Like the one man out of the ten healed of leprosy who came back to give thanks, we need to acknowledge God's graciousness to us.

Second, Jesus' thanksgiving prayer over the food was a prophetic act. Not only was Jesus thanking God for the food already in hand, He was thanking God for the food that was yet to be received. We don't know from the passage if Jesus knew how God would feed all those people, but it is clear that He was certain God would. The same is true for us. When we are entangled in depression or bound by financial needs or physical pain, we don't always know how God will meet our needs. However, we can trust in God's character. We know that He is our Provider and is sufficient in all things. So regardless of how God wants to come and touch us, we can give thanks ahead of time that He will. We don't just give thanks for what God has already done for us. We also thank Him in advance for what we can see prophetically that He will do in our future. When we thank Him for the future blessing, it accelerates that blessing to bring it into our present. Thanksgiving can time travel. It can look into the future and declare thanks now for all that God will do.

After Jesus gave thanks, He also broke the bread. I believe that was more than just a practical act; it was a prophetic act. It symbolized breaking the power of hunger and lack over that crowd of thousands. It broke oppression. We do the same thing with our thanksgiving in worship—we break the power of the oppression over us. We break down the mental strongholds that tie us to lack and attach ourselves to God's goodness. The result of Jesus' prophetic act was a miraculous multiplication of provision. In the same way, as we break the strongholds of the mind that make

God seem small and our problems seem big, we move God's heart. It releases an atmosphere in which miracles can be released.

Another example of God's heart being moved by thanksgiving is found in John 11. This is the story of the death of Lazarus. He and his sisters, Martha and Mary, were dear friends of Jesus. When Lazarus fell ill, the sisters sent a message to Jesus asking Him to come and heal their brother. Jesus assured them that Lazarus wouldn't die, and He continued ministering where He was. After some time, Lazarus did in fact die. Jesus went to His friends, and by that time, Lazarus had been dead for four days.

"Why weren't You here, Jesus?" Martha and Mary asked. "If You had been here, You would have been able to heal him, and he wouldn't have died." They wept in their grief, and they were surrounded by friends who also grieved the tragic death. Jesus was moved to His own sorrow. He groaned and was troubled over the loss of His dear friend and the grief of his sisters. His compassion overwhelmed Him. His grief was so evident that those around Him remarked about how much Jesus must have loved Lazarus. Yet at the same time, the people were confused. Jesus had performed all sorts of miracles and healings. Why didn't He heal His friend? But Jesus knew something that they didn't—God was about to unveil His greatest miracle to date. They had all witnessed Jesus as Healer. They were about to witness Jesus, the Resurrection and the Life.

Still weeping, Jesus walked over to the stone that covered Lazarus's grave and commanded the people to move it out of the way. Mary began to object to Jesus disturbing the body. She couldn't understand what could be gained by unearthing her brother's corpse. The stench of rotting flesh overwhelmed their senses as Jesus walked into the tomb.

"Father," Jesus prayed as He lifted His eyes toward Heaven. "I thank You that You have heard Me. And I know that You always hear Me, but because of the people who are standing by I said this, that they may believe that You sent Me." Then He directed His words to the corpse. "Lazarus!" Jesus cried with a loud voice. "Come forth!" (John 11:41-43). And Lazarus rose from death.

Did you notice what Jesus said just before He raised Lazarus? "Father, I thank You that You have heard Me." In the midst of His groaning and sorrow, in the midst of His compassion, Jesus gave thanks. Even though there seemed little to be thankful for, Jesus began with thanking God for the simplest of matters—He hears Me. Jesus spoke words of thanksgiving bubbling forth from a grateful heart. Thanksgiving turned everything upside down and created an environment for God's Spirit to move and transform death into life.

The worshiper is one who gives thanks in the midst of groaning. Like Jesus, if nothing else, we can be thankful that God hears us. God was prepared to move on Jesus' and Lazarus's behalf, but thanksgiving unlocked the miracle. Thanksgiving moved God's heart to compassion and action. A thankful heart full of faith ignited God's heart and a miracle occurred.

Thanksgiving is a key to unlock the heart of the worshiper and activate the heavenly realm. When we enter His gates with thanksgiving, they open up for us. We speak forth our gratitude, and it breaks off everything bound to that which is not thankful and looses the power of Heaven over us.

We can proclaim our thanks whether we feel like worshiping or not. We give thanks simply because He is worthy of it—not to get anything. We prophetically give thanks as if the blessing has already happened. When we need healing, we thank God for the healing. When we need deliverance from oppression, we thank Him for the freedom before it comes. When we need resources, we thank Him for the provision while still in the place of need. God is already prepared to release what we need from the storehouses of Heaven. Because He loves us!

Praise

The second element of the heart of a worshiper that unlocks the heavenly realms is praise. Praise is important to God; it is so important that 216 verses in the Bible mention it in the context of worship.

Thanksgiving and praise are similar, but there are slight differences. Thanksgiving is a loosing. It's a breaking. It smashes the barrier of unbelief. It's the one-punch that breaks open the atmosphere to God's presence. Praise is the two-punch. It follows thanksgiving and smashes through the impact that thanksgiving initiated.

Psalm 100, which I already referred to, demonstrates this one-two punch: "Enter into His gates with thanksgiving, and into His courts with praise." Thanksgiving takes us through the gates, but praise takes us further into God's courts. Praise places us closer to God's heart, and to a place where His glory and presence abide.

The Hebrew word originally used in that verse for "praise" is *tehillah*. It means a song or hymn of praise, or an act of public praise. This is the key part of the definition: *tehillah* is praise demanded by qualities or deeds or attributes of God, His renown, His fame, and His glory. *Tehillah* praise is linked to God's nature.

The main difference between thanksgiving and praise is what our offering is directed to. Thanksgiving extols God for what He has done or will do. It's connected to His actions. Praise, on the other hand, is demanded by His qualities. When we *tehillah*, we praise God for who He is, His qualities, and His attributes. He embodies each of those qualities whether He ever does anything toward us for which we should be thankful or not. However, because He is love and grace and justice and all the other attributes, He does act on our behalf and we have much to be thankful to Him about.

When we see and taste of God's presence, we can't help but praise. It's the natural response to how lovely He is. It's our innate response, hard-wired into our natures from the time of our creation. It's not something that is demanded of us; we can't help ourselves. We can't *not* praise Him because the qualities and deeds and attributes of God elicit a praise response. The living creatures in Revelation 4 and the seraphim in Isaiah 6 couldn't help themselves from crying "Holy, holy, holy!" Holiness is one of God's attributes; and when we point out how amazing that attribute is, we are engaging in *tehillah*.

I was once part of a large conference service with about 2,000 people in a convention center. We were singing the song "How Great is Our God." As I was leading, I sensed the Lord say to me, "Have them turn." I looked up and saw everyone facing the platform. "Have them turn around and open all the doors to the outside."

There were large sets of double doors all along the back of the room, and we swung them open. We started singing again, "How Great is Our God." Everyone was proclaiming God's great wonders out to the public in a prophetic and intercessory act. It was powerful and the people in the room went crazy declaring God's attributes out into their city.

If you are a worship leader, keep *tehillah* praise in mind when you are selecting your song lists. Choose songs that praise God for His qualities and attributes. You cannot go wrong with songs that praise God. Songs extolling God's mighty nature elicit a responsive expression of God's power. Praise produces power. Power is released when we declare God's wonder, just like when we opened the doors to that convention center. We could feel power going out through those doors. The same release of power happens in our hearts, homes, churches, and nations when we praise God for His attributes.

When the Israelites would go into battle, they would send the singers first. They went before the armies to declare, "The Lord is good and His mercy endures forever!" At times the singers were the only soldiers in the army. But that was all they needed. The praise released God's power and He fought their battles for them. When we praise, we join with the angelic chorus of praise, the heavenly symphony that is already happening all around us. When we join in harmony with the angelic realm, we invoke the host of Heaven's army who are also praising. The Bible states that "angels hearken unto the voice of His word" (see Psalm 103:20). Who gives voice to His word? We do. Angels are activated to the sound of praise; when we agree and declare who He is, our praise produces an open Heaven of honor to God, in which the sounds of Heaven mingle with the sounds of earth to release His power.

The only weapon we need to fight the battles in our lives is the weapon of praise. Psalm 149:6 tells us to let the high praises of God be on our lips, and a two-edged sword be in our hands. It's our declaration of praise mingled with His word that becomes a mighty sword that cuts through the atmosphere creating an open Heaven all around us. Each believer carries a song of praise, a hymn, or a spiritual song. Release it publicly and extol the attributes of God. It will strike down every oppression and launch you into your destiny.

The great news is that praise is a beautiful sound no matter who sings it. You don't have to be the best singer to praise God for His attributes. If only the best birds in the forest sang, the forests would be very quiet places. God created all of us to sing and make melody in our hearts. The heart is the source of praise, not the mouth or vocal cords. The voice is just the medium through which praise flows.

In fact, the voice is only one medium of many through which sound can travel. You don't even have to sing to praise. Another word for "praise" used in the Bible is *yadah*. It means to extend your hand as a blessing. When we raise our hands and bless the Lord, we are displaying *yadah* praise. It is praise pouring out through our hands. Our extended hands make a sound too, even if we don't hear it. You can also praise His attributes through quiet prayer or the arts. You can paint, dance, or write His praises. There are infinite ways to praise, so it doesn't matter how we do it as long as we just do it. God made each person unique with different personalities. Your praise will look different from mine. That is part of the beauty that makes up the tapestry of sound lifted to honor God.

Another word for "praise," which I love, is *zamar*. Psalm 147:7 uses *zamar*: "Sing to the Lord with thanksgiving, sing praises [zamar] on the harp to our God." *Zamar* means to sing, to praise, to make music, to play musical instruments, or to strike the strings. It's to worship through instruments.

When I lead worship, I often transition into times of musical interlude. It's a very deliberate choice. I'm not just looking for the right key to play or passing time until I figure out what to do. I'm *zamar*-ing. We play our praise through our instruments.

While *zamar* is done on an instrument, it is so much richer than just playing music. Praise flowing forth through sound can sometimes speak so much more than our vocabulary can. We are limited in our vocabulary, but *zamar* crafts praise in a way that supersedes what our words are capable of.

That verse in Psalm 147 says to sing our praise on our instruments. It instructs us to sing with a harp. So when you play your instrument, you are singing. You declare God's attributes through the music.

There's also a difference between just playing your instrument and *zamar*-ing. You can play artfully and never *zamar*. *Zamar* is an act of praise. You can play the same notes, but they sound different when they are played in praise. They are richer, fuller, and alive. They sing. The difference between the two is that the notes are flowing through the heart of the worshiper with *zamar*. When a worshiper plays, you connect in the Spirit with fluidity and dynamics and modulations that transcend the notes on a page.

A very clear connection can be seen between *zamar* and singing in tongues. They both transcend the mind, surpass the limits of language, and release the Spirit and mysteries. First Corinthians 14:2 tells us, "For he who speaks in a tongue does not speak to men but to God, for no one understands him; however, in the spirit he speaks mysteries." That definition of tongues is very similar to the definition of *zamar*. They both release mysteries and free up your mind. When we sing in the Spirit and when we *zamar*, our bodies and souls get out of the way. All that's left is our spirit singing directly to God's Spirit. You don't have to think about the next word or figure anything out. The sound just bubbles up from the overflow of the heart.

When the whole congregation joins together to sing in the Spirit or sing the song of the Lord, it sounds like many waters to me. Jesus said, "He who believes in Me... out of his heart will flow rivers of living water" (John 7:38). There's a river in each one of us waiting to come out. When it does, it's absolutely beautiful. It's the sound of praise to God stripped of the entrapments of the flesh.

The final psalms depict some beautiful ways to *zamar* and enter into praise. Beginning with Psalm 149:1-3, "Praise the Lord! Sing to the Lord a new song, and His praise in the assembly of saints. Let Israel rejoice in their Maker; let the children of Zion be joyful in their King. Let them praise His name with the dance. Let them sing praises to Him with the timbrel and the harp." Praise flows through dance and the harp. The guitars we use today are simple derivatives of the ancient harps. So when we play guitar, we are obeying the commands to sing praises to God through the harp.

Psalm 150 lists all the different instruments we are commanded to praise God with, including the harps, timbrel, stringed instruments, trumpets, and cymbals. I love the cymbal part because it tells me Jesus loves percussion! The people who believe that we shouldn't use guitars and drums in worship are misled in their belief that God doesn't want those kinds of sounds. God created all sounds, and He loves it when we worship Him through our instruments.

The final phrase of Psalm 150 is "Let everything that has breath praise the Lord." That word for "praise" is *halal*, which means to rave, to boast, to shine, to celebrate, and to be clamorously foolish. Clamorously foolish—I love that! When we abandon ourselves to praising God, we will look foolish to the world. But that foolishness leads us to decrease so that Christ can increase in us. First Corinthians 1:27 states, "But God has chosen the foolish things of the world to put to shame the wise, and God has chosen the weak things of the world to put to shame the things which are mighty." Our clamorous foolishness will confound those who are lost, but it brings honor and glory to God. When we glorify Him upon our praises, He is magnified high above any other name, and His power is shown.

Worship

The third key to releasing the heavenly sound is worship. Thanksgiving comes first, then praise, then worship. They build upon each other. Psalm 5:7 says, "As for me, in the abundance of your loving kindness, I will come into your house with thanksgiving and praise. And I will bow down toward your holy temple in reverence of you" (paraphrased).

Thanksgiving and praise are the first steps that lead us to bowing down in reverence. That is worship. The phrase for "bowing down" in this verse is *barak*. It means to kneel as an act of blessing. That blessing can occur in two directions. First, we bow down in an act of humility to bless

God. When we kneel, we make ourselves low. This is what happens when we worship. We make ourselves low as we lift Him higher upon our praise. Lavish worship exalts Him higher, and we can't help but diminish in light of His worth. We often physically kneel as a representation of this lowering so that He may be exalted.

In the psalms it says, "Oh come, let us worship and bow down; let us kneel before the Lord our Maker" (Psalm 95:6). "Oh, worship the Lord in the beauty of holiness! Tremble before Him, all the earth" (Psalm 96:9). We worship *(barak)* the Lord in the beauty of His holiness. When we come to understand and meditate upon His holiness, we can't help but respond in worship. The gravity of His holiness evokes our bowing to Him in that place of encounter.

There's a second action that often happens when we *barak*. It's a spiritual principle that Jesus describes in His exhortation to His disciples: "Whoever...is least among you all will be great" (Luke 9:48). Though we never seek to be lifted up when we exalt God, it's an unintended consequence of our praise. This is the second direction of blessing when we bow. When medieval knights were honored with their title, they would bow so they could receive a blessing. Sometimes we make ourselves low and *barak* and we are the ones who are blessed.

When we reach that place of encounter with the Spirit, we are engrossed in praising Him for His deeds, His attributes, and His might. We have completely abandoned ourselves and made ourselves humble before him. James 4:10 admonishes us, "Humble yourselves in the sight of the Lord, and He will lift you up."

When we kneel down before God in reverence to Him, He sees that submission and obedience and responds with honor. He lifts our heads up, and He speaks to us face to face. That's what I call the place of encounter. It's the place where His glory and presence fill the atmosphere and we have each other's full attention. That's the place I live for. That's where we want to go in our worship. It's the place of just loving on God. We foolishly, clamorously adore Him, and He pours His love right back into us.

Even when we aren't feeling worship, we can enter into a place of encounter. There are times we "faith it" instead of "feel it." We *choose* to draw near to God through thanksgiving, praise, and worship. James 4:8 tells us to draw near to God and He will draw near to us. So we can stand on that word and trust that as we give God our worship in faith, He will draw near to us. Sometimes all we can do is stand upon the Word. We don't feel joyful. We don't feel like worshiping, but we do it as an act of faith, knowing that He is worthy of our praise. Faith can supersede our weaknesses. It transcends our physical ailments and limitations. It reaches past the bondages and oppression in which we may be entangled. Faith trumps feeling when it is aligned with God's Word. When we stand on the truth of God's Word, God sees our faith and responds in compassion. He lifts us up and brings us to a place of encounter.

I love the "suddenly moments." The suddenly moments are when it seems like nothing is happening. If we trust our feelings, we would think God is not near. But we stand on the truth of the Word and persevere in worship. When we do, He suddenly breaks through to our awareness and encounters us with His glory.

Encounter is all about relationship. You can't have a relationship with someone without encountering or experiencing them. I can know all about the president of the United States. I can know his birthplace, hobbies, political stances, and family background. I can quote all his stats and recount pointless trivia from his life. But I don't really have a relationship with him until I've had an encounter with him. It's one thing to say, "The president likes to go jogging," and it's another thing altogether to put on your shoes and run a 5K next to him. As you run, you talk about what's going on in his life and the matters that are important to him. There's no relationship without encounter, and the same principle applies to our relationship with God. He doesn't want you to just know about Him, quote all His stats, and recite all His favorite verses. He wants to encounter you, touch you, and be touched by you. It's radically different from just knowing about Him.

A fallacy is often promoted in the church that sounds something like this: "Too much Spirit and you are going to blow up. Too much Word and you are going to dry up." People warn about becoming too experience-oriented. I wonder how it's possible to be too experience-oriented. How can we experience too much of God? How is it possible to have too much of the Word? I want to be experience-oriented. I want to be Word-oriented. I don't have to give up one in order to have the other.

Secrets can only be heard up close. When we are in a place of encounter, God draws us up close to His heart. There are revelations we can receive only in that place of encounter. For example, I never would have understood the swirling sounds of creation all around us if I hadn't had that encounter about Revelation 4 and the crickets. God spoke His secrets to me in that place of encounter, and when I share those secrets with other people, that dimension is opened for them. There are times when God whispers things to my heart and I think, *Wow! I never knew that before!* It's because I had never been that close before.

God delights to tell us His secrets. He loves to give us pleasure. "Delight yourself also in the Lord, and He shall give you the desires of your heart" (Psalm 37:4). It's a nice exchange. We delight in God just because He's lovely. But He loves us so much that He wants to give to us as well. The more we do this, the more the overwhelming desire of our heart is to touch His heart again. So there's a cycle of desiring Him, delighting in Him, and desiring Him even more. It's a continuous circle of encounter, a masterful dance of divine romance.

Delight is the bottom line of worship. When we worship, all our delight is wrapped up in doing His pleasure and lifting Him up. When He is our delight, obedience is a joy! Rather than obedience being a drudgery, we chase after the opportunity to follow Him wherever He leads. Honor, praise, adoration, and obedience become our pleasure.

And He loves to give us more of Him. It's like watching young children Christmas morning. They excitedly rip open the paper from the presents, get frustrated when they can't open the box fast enough, and tear into the packaging to find that treasure. As a parent, I know the feeling of watching my children and anticipating that moment. We carefully select the perfect gift, wrap it in their favorite color of paper, and expectantly await their reaction to the gift. I'm not sure who gets the most pleasure out of that moment, the child who receives the gift or the parent who delights in watching their child experience so much joy.

How much more does our Father delight in us when we experience the gifts that He has for us! We tear into His gifts, His secrets, His presence, and He gleams with pride over His kids. When we worship, He reveals His secrets to our hearts. As they permeate into our spirits, He rejoices, "Yes! She got it!" And the revelation produces simultaneous growth and hunger for more. The delight cycle swirls faster and deeper.

There are also times when He lets us search Him out. He waits to see how hungry we are for His presence, how thirsty we are for revelation. As we search Him out, His heart is moved and he shows us His secrets. He shows us His heart. Proverbs 25:2 tells us, "It is the glory of God to conceal a matter, but the glory of kings is to search out a matter." That's the essence of worship: it's a game of hide and seek for the Father's heart.

And here's the amazing twist: the revelation isn't just for us. We can share it! The secrets God reveals to our hearts can be a testimony that releases the same revelation over someone else's life. Our encounter and intimacy with Christ can destroy the bondages over someone else. We can sing our encounter over someone and it becomes their song of deliverance.

The same keys that bring us into God's presence— thanksgiving, praise, and worship—are also keys to loose God's presence over others. God's encounters with us become the breakthrough for others. We can use the weapons of thanksgiving, praise, and worship to usher in God's presence into our lives. He delights to war on our behalf for the benefit of others when we enter into worship. We should also never forget that we can release those blessings gained in intimacy with God over others. We can give thanks, praise, and worship on behalf of our family to loose the power of God in their lives. We can release the Spirit of God into our cities and our nation.

Worship and intercession are two keys for the same lock. We worship and Satan's strongholds are destroyed. When God's glory comes, we are transformed. As sons and daughters of God we have the authority to release His presence into the atmosphere. Families are transformed through thanksgiving. Cities come alive under the garment of praise. Nations tremble as we worship the

King of kings. The weapons we possess are mighty, and they release the power of God to bring about His purposes on the earth.

CHAPTER 5

A PRIESTHOOD OF WORSHIPERS

One of the functions of a worshiper is to be a priest. Revelation 5 tells us that God has made us to be kings and priests unto Him (see Revelation 5:10). We can better understand how worship works when we understand our role as priests. That sounds terribly heady, but it's not really. It's best understood when we understand what it means to be a priest.

In the Old Testament, God established priests as the liaisons between the people and God. They would bring the sacrifices before the Lord. They would offer up the sacrificed oils, grains, incense, and animals to atone for the sins of the people. The offerings also included sacrifices of thanks and praise for the deeds of God. The priests were the only ones allowed access into the Holy of Holies where God's presence dwelled.

The priests also served as representatives. They would represent the people to God, and they represented God to the people. They mediated between humankind and God. The priests would beseech God for blessing on behalf of the people.

Under the Old Covenant, only a small number of people were designated as priests. Even among the priesthood, only the high priest was allowed to enter the Holy of Holies, and that was only permitted once a year on the Day of Atonement. A thick veil separated God's presence confined within the Holy of Holies from the people outside the temple.

When Jesus died upon the cross, He offered the ultimate sacrifice. He offered His own pure, unblemished blood. His shed blood rendered the definitive atonement for the sin of all humankind. His blood was much more powerful than that of any sheep or bull. It had the power to atone for all sin once for all, and the need for any single priest was abolished the instant of His sacrifice. At the moment of His death, the veil that separated the Holy of Holies from the people was ripped in two.

Jesus became the ultimate High Priest. He embodied the sacrifice required for our sin. No priest would ever again be able to present any sacrifice that could compare to what Jesus had accomplished.

Yet First Peter 2 calls those who follow Christ a priesthood. Why would we be called priests when Jesus already fulfilled the ultimate role of priest? Because we are still called to be ones who present sacrifices to God. The difference is these sacrifices don't atone for our sin. Jesus already did that. The sacrifice we give is a life laid down in devotion to God. The sacrifice is ourselves.

The word "priest" can evoke an image of a lofty, unrelatable person with consecrated garments that set the priest apart from the rest of the people. However, the priest of the New Covenant is completely opposite of that image. As the priesthood of believers, we are called to a place of lowness, a place of submission and consecration to God. While outer garments once set priests apart from the crowd, it is now a life of submission that sets a priest apart. It's a distinction that is less obvious to the eye but even more powerful in the heavenly realms.

The simplest definition of priest is "one who offers spiritual sacrifices." First Peter 2:5 says, "You also, as living stones, are being built up a spiritual house, a holy priesthood, to offer up spiritual sacrifices acceptable to God through Jesus Christ." From this verse we learn that the priestly function of our worship is to offer spiritual sacrifices.

Paul pleads in Romans 12:1, "I beseech you therefore, brethren, by the mercies of God, that you present your bodies a living sacrifice, holy, acceptable to God, which is your reasonable service." Our service to God is to present ourselves as living sacrifices. Dead animals can't praise God. Yet a living, breathing, laid-down life is the ultimate offering of worship to Him.

SUBMISSION TO GOD

James 4:7 tells us to submit ourselves to God. The primary function of a priest is to submit to God. A sacrificed life is a submitted life. It has been consecrated—committed—to God's service. Your spiritual sacrifice is your life laid bare, cracked open, and offered as incense before the Lord. Physical sacrifices of animals and crops and incense are no longer of value. Our sacrifice is a *spiritual* one. It's our spirit. It is an offering of all of who we are—dedicated to God.

Jesus told the woman at the well in John chapter 4 that the true worshipers will worship the Father in spirit and in truth. They worship God with their laid-down lives led by sensitive-to-the-movements of the Spirit. They also worship God with their lives submitted to the Word of God. True priests value both the Word and the Spirit. They pursue and submit to both with abandon.

Jesus Himself lived a submitted life. He did everything in obedience to the Father. In fact, Jesus stated in John 5:19, "Most assuredly, I say to you, the Son can do nothing of Himself, but what He sees the Father do; for whatever He does, the Son also does in like manner." Jesus only did what He saw the Father doing; nothing more and nothing less. That is a life completely submitted to the Father.

As priests, we too are submitted because we no longer seek our own will but the will of the Father. As Paul states in Galatians 2:20, the life we live does not even belong to us anymore: "I have been crucified with Christ; it is no longer I who live, but Christ lives in me; and the life which I now live in the flesh I live by faith in the Son of God, who loved me and gave Himself for me." You can't be any more submitted than to no longer allow yourself to live and instead live by faith in the Son of God who loves us.

James 4:7-8 continues, "Therefore submit to God. Resist the devil and he will flee from you. Draw near to God and He will draw near to you. Cleanse your hands, you sinners; and purify your hearts, you double-minded." A second function of a priest is to resist the devil. Our greatest weapon in resisting the devil is submission to God. When we submit to God, the enemy has no hold over us.

I love the third function of a priest described by James: "Draw near to God and He will draw near to you." It's an instruction tied to a promise. We draw near to Him. That in itself is absolutely lovely. I desire to spend all eternity drawing near to God. But that He promises to draw near to us in response is amazing! God's reciprocating devotion is humbling and endearing.

The fourth function of a priest James mentions is to cleanse and purify ourselves from double-mindedness. God is looking for single-minded affection. Like the dove's eyes in Song of Solomon, we seek to look only upon Him. Worship evokes this amazing ability to fix our eyes on Him. We often become double-minded without even being cognizant that it has happened. We slip into it. Like a bent tire rim on a bicycle, unless we intentionally keep our eyes going forward, we will slowly meander off track. Like the deviations from the footprint of our destiny, we tend to stray because our eyes wander without our awareness. But worship brings us back to center. It focuses our eyes, and that aligns our whole beings, in a forward direction leading only to God. Worship aligns us with our destiny simply because it keeps our eyes directed to Jesus.

Priests in the Old Covenant had a special privilege that was unique to their role: they were the only ones who were permitted near God's presence. I'm so glad that we live in this time of the New Covenant when we are all priests who can all enter into the Holy of Holies of God's indwelling presence. Psalm 73:28 gives us the key to joy in worship: "But it is good for me to draw near to God: I have put my trust in the Lord God, that I may declare all thy works" (KJV). Once again we are reminded that our joy comes from one Source: our nearness to God. Apart from Him, there is no joy.

JOY IN HIS PRESENCE

Need a little pick-me-up? Draw near to God and He will draw near to you. Your joy is in the nearness. I love that! When I'm dry, I know I must get in God's presence. Like the psalmist in Psalm 42:1, "As the deer pants for the water brooks, so my soul longs for You, O God." Nothing satisfies like God's nearness.

I lead worship in a lot of places, and I get to play with a lot of teams. Occasionally, I guest lead a church in which the worship team seems a little parched. They could use an infusion of some joy. I actually see it a lot, and it saddens me. I notice that people often get caught in the never-satisfying cycle of trying to do all the right things at the right time just to be free. But it never works. The only way we experience joy is to stop trying to get it all right and just draw near to God. Of course we are to be skillful in our approach, but the bottom line is connecting with Him. If you lead worship, take a good look at your team. Do they look joyful? If not, focus on drawing near to God in worship.

The end of Psalm 73 states that we take refuge in Him that we may tell all what He has done. There is a calling we have as priests. Not only do we lay down our lives in submission to God, we are also proclaimers. We are the ones who bellow forth a proclamation of God's goodness. It bubbles forth from the overflow of the place of joy.

When we worship we declare God's wonders. On one hand, it's an act of devotion and adoration to God. On the other, it also serves as a proclamation to others. When we sing, "God, You are holy. You are lovely. Your ways are higher than our ways," we are functioning in our calling to tell all what He has done.

As priests, we also petition God on behalf of our brothers and sisters. We represent them to God. Part of a worship leader's function is to capture the heart of the congregation and offer it up to God as the sacrifice. To be able to connect with your church's heartbeat is a skill in itself. It creates unity and a point of identification for everyone in the room, "Hey, that's exactly how I feel" is what you want your people to say to themselves. A great song will do the same thing.

Jesus is our access point into the Holy of Holies. It was His shed blood that rent the veil of separation in two. Through Him we access God's presence and we declare its availability to those around us who are lost, hurting, and oppressed. Hebrews 10:19-22 states:

> *Therefore, brethren, having boldness to enter the Holiest by the blood of Jesus, by a new and living way which He consecrated for us, through the veil, that is, His flesh, and having a High Priest over the house of God, let us draw near with a true heart in full assurance of faith, having our hearts sprinkled from an evil conscience and our bodies washed with pure water.*

Once again in this verse, we see the priestly themes of consecration, drawing near to God, and purity. We can draw near to God with a true heart in full assurance of faith. We will never be rebuked by God for drawing near. We can do so with full assurance of faith. We don't have to worship God from afar. We become dry and parched when we try to worship from afar. That's a works mentality that says, "I have to do this for God." You can't earn anything from Him—it's already given! You can't make Him love you more—He already does! Many times we forget that He delights in our presence and invites us to draw near. We can approach the throne of grace with confidence because we have been invited.

God is enthroned on our praises. He inhabits the praises of His people! When we lift our voices to Him in worship, our praise forms a resting place for Him to sit upon. When we need His presence and we can't go any further without it, construct a place for Him to abide and be seated. In essence we are building a throne for Him to inhabit. The throne's legs are constructed of "Hallelujah," and the cushion is crafted with "You are worthy." Piece by piece, our praise erects a throne worthy of His presence. Our access isn't through the blood of lambs. It's through Jesus and a life laid down in praise to Him.

Priests have access to God's presence. They are the ones granted permission to enter the Holy of Holies. Because of Jesus' sacrifice, the "No Trespassing" sign on the doorpost of the Holy of Holies has been replaced with "Access Granted." It's because we are seated together with Christ in the heavenly places (see Ephesians 2:6-7). He's already made the way for us.

THREE REQUIREMENTS

Love

There are three requirements of the priesthood: love, obedience, and humility. The first requirement is love. When Jesus was asked what the greatest commandment was, He replied, "Love the Lord, your God, with all your heart, soul, and mind. The second is like unto it, love your neighbor as yourself" (Matthew 22:37-39, paraphrased). The greatest action a worshiper can pursue is to love. It is out of our love for God that the sweet fragrance of worship flows. As we ascend to the heavenly places in love and devotion to

God, we are filled to overflowing and can then love others as ourselves. I call it the splat factor. The priesthood enters God's presence through the gateway of love. We fall splat into His presence where we get infused with even more love. Then, splat, we come back to earth and squish out love on everybody else. As we pour ourselves out in love to God, we become like a sponge that can then soak up more and more of His presence, which overflows as love on those around us. Loving your neighbor is the by-product of loving God. When you connect with His heart for humanity you begin to see through His eyes, and how He looks at all of us as His sons and daughters.

Love isn't a sterile emotion. It's not impotent. It's active, lavish, and passionate. When we love on God, it should be passionate. Leaders, if you want to lead people where you are going, you have to be passionate. We don't just appreciate God and worship Him from the place of moderated respect. No, we are voraciously in love with the God who loves us extravagantly and furiously. People will only go as far in worship as you go. So if your love is lacking in luster, draw near to Him. Allow Him to stir your affections for Him. It's okay if people don't follow you at first. That's the nature of being a leader. Leaders take people where they would not normally go on their own. Devote yourself to a life of extravagant love, and others will follow your lead. When we love God passionately, He loves right back on us. That's the nearness that infuses us with joy. Joy makes us smile, and smiles are contagious. So be patient with your people. If they aren't following yet, just keep running harder after God and soon you will stir them to jealousy.

Obedience

Love is the first requirement of a priest, and obedience is the second. Jeremiah 7:23 commands us, "Obey My voice, and I will be your God, and you shall be My people. And walk in all the ways that I have commanded you, that it may be well with you." Obedience is our service to God. It's the submission of a consecrated life. You can't be submitted without also being obedient.

Obedience gets a bad rap, and is often misunderstood. For some reason, obedience gets equated with being required to do something awful. Granted, obedience is a sacrifice, and all sacrifice costs us something. However, obedience is just another way of saying, "God I trust that Your wisdom surpasses mine. I want to go left, but if You say right, I'm going to trust that right is right." When we are traversing that destiny-journey God has us on, it is obedience that keeps us on track. When we step out of obedience, we stray off the path of our God-gifted destiny. Obedience is a gift from God and it's a gift for God. That's why obedience is better than sacrifice (see 1 Samuel 15:22). Sacrifices can be given without giving your heart, but obedience is the sacrifice of the heart.

I love that Jeremiah 7:23 commands obedience, then it immediately promises our fulfillment. When we walk in obedience, He promises to be our God and make all to be well with us. God doesn't have to give back to us, but He delights in giving us pleasure.

Humility

The third requirement of a priest is humility. The prophet Micah beautifully describes this principle: "He has shown you, O man, what is good; and what does the Lord require of you but to do justly, to love mercy [goodness and kindness], and to walk humbly [modestly and showing humility] with your God?" (Micah 6:8).

Humility was embodied in the life of Jesus. He humbled Himself to leave His heavenly throne and become a human. He humbled Himself to serve, heal, and restore the very humanity who had rejected Him. He humbled Himself by permitting His own children to kill Him. If He is our High Priest, then we follow His path of humility when we become priests as well.

To lead is to serve. Leadership is not a position of authority as much as it is a position of humility. If you are a worship leader, your primary goal is not for people to follow you. It is to serve. It's the position of humility. Worship leaders should serve on at least four planes. *First,* you serve God. Your worship leading is in submission to Him first. *Second,* if you lead within the context of a local church, you are there to serve the worship vision of your pastor. It requires humility to follow someone else's vision for your role, especially if you have a difference of opinion. If you don't know your pastor's vision, ask, "Can we take some time to sit down together and develop a vision for worship? I'm here to serve you and facilitate your vision for the church and do that through the worship ministry. I want to make sure I lead in a way that serves your leadership."

Third, you are to serve your team. Your role as leader includes equipping them to excel in their gifts. If you think they are just there to make you look good, then you are not serving and you are not leading. You are to do what you can to facilitate their growth in their musicianship, their leadership, and their worship. So how does that happen? Rehearsals are the best place to build team and release those into their giftings. There is no pressure of a Sunday meeting. Sure you need to learn new songs, but if that's all you do, you will kill the creativity of your team. Take time to "jam with the Lamb." When your team can feel comfortable to explore and try new things, it will breathe life into your worship and create creative synergy. Synergy is so important, it's the dynamic of music—it's the dance of the Spirit flowing through each member of the team. And if you keep practicing that, you will find that your team can go places in the spirit that you've never been before. There has to be dialog in the music. That comes from listening to what everyone else is playing and responding through the language of music.

Fourth, a worship leader should seek to serve the body by bringing them into a place of worship. It's not really worship leading if we don't serve them by teaching them how to worship and giving them opportunities to experience God through worship. They can only go as far as you go, so bring them as far as you can take them. Help them turn their affections to Jesus. Help them forget what they are going through, and point them to Jesus. That is an act of service.

THE ALTAR OF WORSHIP

Humility is a mark of a laid-down life. It's the living sacrifice lifestyle. I was pondering this one day when I started thinking about the stage that most churches have. It's the place where we stand when we lead worship. It's the raised area in the room that allows for sight lines for people in the back to see. That's its physical function. I was pondering the stage one day, and I thought to myself, *"Stage" sounds like a performance.* No doubt you've heard, "Can we have the worship team please come to the stage?" So I religified it. *This sounds better,* I thought, "Can I have the worship team come up to the platform?" *Yes much better.* I could sense the Lord chuckling as He spoke to my spirit, "It's not a stage. It's not a platform. It's an altar. That's where you go to be sacrificed. That's where you lay down your life." The second we place our feet on that altar, we die to ourselves. If we could just grasp that one concept, our worship would be transformed.

When we step on the stage, it's not a platform for people to see us better. It's an altar—the place where sacrifices are made, where we lay ourselves out as lambs to the slaughter. That's the priesthood! It's the sacrificed life. Some platforms are tricked out with lights and smoke and mirrors, and there's nothing wrong with that. But when the rubber meets the road, it's just a box unless there's a sacrifice on it. It only becomes an altar when we bare ourselves open as sacrifices before God. It doesn't matter if that altar is in a dirt shack in Mozambique or the fanciest cathedral in the United States. The presence of a sacrifice is what determines whether it's an altar or not. Once you are laid out as a sacrifice on the altar, you are His to do with as He pleases. Leading worship is about Him, not you. He can choose to do whatever He wants to do in the service.

Sacrifices aren't born on stages. You can't live your life whichever way you please off the stage then suddenly become a sacrifice the moment you step onto the platform. That's not a life of obedience and consecration. That's not the priesthood. That's a falsehood and a performance. We live our lives in submission and humility. Then nothing changes when we step onto the stage. We've just transitioned from the altar of everyday life to the altar behind a microphone. No difference. When we are on the altar, it's like God cracks us open. What comes out is what has been there all along. We open up ourselves and make ourselves vulnerable, and what is released is the same sacrifice we live every day. That's consecration. That is priesthood.

When we are a life laid bare, we desire no recognition of our own. We seek only to ascribe honor to Jesus. Psalm 29 says, "Ascribe to the Lord, O heavenly beings, ascribe to the Lord glory and strength. Ascribe to the Lord the glory due his name" (Psalm 29:1-2 ESV). "Ascribe" is a cool word. It means to "attach" something. Attach attributes to God. We ascribe glory and strength to God.

I was in a service once when I was meditating on that Scripture, *God, what does it look like to ascribe glory to You?*

Then I had a picture in my mind. I saw people in worship. As they were worshiping, they lifted up their hands. God was standing before them in a beautiful robe. The people were attaching words of honor to His robe. Glory. Beauty. Honor. Blessings. Holiness. Righteousness. Word after word, the people were ascribing Him glory by pinning the words to His robe. It was such a beautiful picture of worship. That's what we do in worship. He is robed in the honor we ascribe to Him. He is seated on the throne of praise that we build for Him. And He just radiates there in His beauty. He becomes more and more beautiful as we ascribe more honor to Him.

DWELLING WITH HIM

My life Scripture is Psalm 27:4. I write it down everywhere. It's all over my house. "One thing have I desired of the Lord, that will I seek: that I may dwell in the house of the Lord all the days of my life, to behold the beauty of the Lord, and to inquire in His temple." The one thing the priest seeks is to dwell in the house of the Lord. I'm more at home in His house than in any house I could ever own. It's what I seek: God's presence. Wherever He is, is where I want to be. I want to dwell in that place all the days of my life. Yesterday's revelation won't sustain me through today. I must dwell in God's presence today and every day for all the days of my life.

We seek to dwell in His presence so we can "behold the beauty of the Lord and to inquire in His temple." When we are in that posture of ascribing glory to God and attaching honor to Him, He invites us to inquire of Him. We draw near to Him and He draws near to us, and we have the freedom to inquire of Him.

"Lord, what would You have me do about this situation?"

"Love your neighbor."

"Lord, what would You have me do about that?"

"Just love Me and watch what I do."

Oh the beauty of conversation with God! The freedom to inquire of Him! Oh yes, and by the way, He hasn't stopped speaking!

All the cares of the world are stripped away as we nestle close to His heart and He draws near. We make our goal to enter into a place of worship in which we delight in His nearness. We meditate on His beauty, gaze up at Him, and contemplate His wonders. His glory comes, and it overflows with satisfaction and joy. When you lead others into that place, anything can happen because there are no limits.

There are no barriers in the glory. No limitations. Power is released to overcome every obstacle. All that's left to do in the glory is just to bask. Enjoy it. Soak it up like a sponge—then take the overflow with you and leak everywhere you go.

CHAPTER 6

THE PSALMIST'S ANOINTING

There are dimensions of worship. Worship has colors and shapes. One dimension of worship is the priesthood. That's when we offer ourselves as sacrifices for God's service. We lay ourselves down on the altar of sacrifice to God. The priesthood contributes the sound of submission and humility to Heaven's symphony.

Another dimension of worship is the psalmist's anointing. It carries a different weight—a different texture—than the priesthood. It's the sound of power. It's the *dunamis* of worship. While the priesthood's role is in service and vulnerability, the function of the psalmist's anointing is in power and the glory.

The priesthood's weapons are meekness, humility, and service; the psalmist's anointing is a sword fashioned to build and destroy. The psalmist's anointing changes circumstances. It breaks. It shatters strongholds. It builds a resting place for God's glory, and it destroys the schemes of the enemy to steal glory from God. It functions in healing, deliverance, and the establishment of atmospheres pregnant with God's voice. It fosters an environment suitable for God to move in power and demonstrate His might.

Isaiah 61:1 says, "The Spirit of the Lord God is upon Me because the Lord has anointed Me to preach good tidings to the poor; He has sent Me to heal the brokenhearted, to proclaim liberty to the captives, and the opening of the prison to those who are bound." This passage was historically interpreted as being Messianic. It foretells of Jesus and describes what the Anointed One will do and look like. When Jesus began His earthly ministry, He went to a synagogue, pulled out a scroll of Isaiah, and read this passage (see Luke 4:18-19). He was declaring that He was the Anointed One. He was the One who would preach good news, bind up the brokenhearted, and proclaim liberty to the captives. He was telling us His job description. He was saying, "I'm the Anointed One, and this is what the Anointed One does: destroys darkness and brings forth the kingdom of God."

Jesus did all the things described in Isaiah 61. The blind were healed. Those bound in spiritual bondage were loosed from their oppression. The lame walked. The lepers were restored. The dead were raised. In Matthew 10, Jesus instructed the disciples to continue His ministry of power, "Proclaim the message that the kingdom of God is at hand. Heal the sick, cleanse the lepers, raise the dead, and cast out demons." That's what a disciple does—follows in the footsteps of the master. In other words, as Jesus' disciples, we are called and commissioned to continue Jesus' job description of Isaiah 61.

Matthew 28:19-20 further instructs us in the Great Commission to perpetuate His ministry by being disciples who make more disciples. So all disciples, even you and I today, should look like Jesus. We should look like powerful bondage-breaking, freedom-releasing, sickness-healing, kingdom-declaring anointed ones.

Jesus foretold what the future anointed ones would look like. "Greater works than these [you] will do, because I go to My Father" (John 14:12). His anointing didn't stop when He ascended to Heaven. And remarkably, He didn't just leave the role of carrying the anointing and the ministry of power on the Holy Spirit to continue. The Holy Spirit would be our Helper and Guide as Jesus called humans to be the ones to carry the anointing. He became the Head and we became His body. As His body, we continue the works of Christ, even to a greater measure than what Jesus saw during His earthly ministry.

THE ANOINTING'S POWER

The anointing brings power. That power rests on you. Every believer carries the anointing. If the Anointed One, Jesus, lives in you, then you have the anointing. We are all anointed. We stand in the gap for all who are oppressed, and we possess the power to release them from bondage.

God's power can be manifested in many ways. It can release in the form of physical healing. God's power can heal wounded emotions and hearts. Demons flee in the anointing, and people are set free from lifelong addictions, lies, and bondage. Chains are loosed. Generational curses are destroyed. The anointing can create an atmosphere for the prophetic word of the Lord to speak edification and encouragement to people who are distraught and without hope. It unleashes freedom for all who are oppressed by the enemy's snares. Miracles are released in the anointing. When we share or sing testimonies of God's power, it releases a Spirit of prophecy so that others can experience the same power.

The psalmist's anointing is simply the ability to release the power of the presence of God and the Word of the Lord into the atmosphere through music. I don't have any power on my own. I don't carry healing around in my pockets or tucked between the keys on my keyboard. I can't loose someone from bondage on my own. But when I join in with Heaven's symphony of worship and declare God's wonders, I am sowing into an atmosphere of glory in which God's power can be demonstrated. God is the One who heals, sets free, and redeems. However, He often chooses to do those things through human vessels. It's the psalmists' anointing that makes that possible. We all have the psalmist anointing. The key is to learn how to release it in order for power to be demonstrated.

My understanding of the psalmist's anointing was refined and forged in my hours at the little Spinet piano at

Rachel's house. Even though Rachel's ultimate healing came when she went to be with the Lord, we experienced many mini-breakthroughs of healing along the way. Though her tumor grew, God's power to release His presence and make His glory manifest was often thick in the room. At Rachel's house I learned the art of creating atmosphere for God's presence to rest upon.

The psalmist is one who fosters the anointing. By creating an atmosphere of worship, we allow God's presence to come and release in power. A beautiful example of this is found in Second Kings chapter 3. King Jehoshaphat was reigning, and the Israelite armies were in trouble. While out on an excursion, they had run out of water in the desert. The Israelite soldiers, their horses, and all their livestock were in danger of dying. Not only were they dying of thirst, but they were also vulnerable to attack from the Moabites. If the armies were defeated, it could bring destruction upon the entire nation of Israel. Read what happened next in Second Kings 3:11-15:

> But Jehoshaphat said, "Is there no prophet of the Lord here, that we may inquire of the Lord by him?" So one of the servants of the king of Israel answered and said, "Elisha the son of Shaphat is here, who poured water on the hands of Elijah." And Jehoshaphat said, "The word of the Lord is with him." So the king of Israel and Jehoshaphat and the king of Edom went down to him. Then Elisha said to the king of Israel, "What have I to do with you? Go to the prophets of your father

and the prophets of your mother." But the king of Israel said to him, "No, for the Lord has called these three kings together to deliver them into the hand of Moab." And Elisha said, "As the Lord of hosts lives, before whom I stand, surely were it not that I regard the presence of Jehoshaphat king of Judah, I would not look at you, nor see you. But now bring me a musician." Then it happened, when the musician played, that the hand of the Lord came upon him. And he said, "Thus says the Lord: 'Make this valley full of ditches.'"

Do you see what happened there? The king inquired of the prophet for direction, and Elisha basically said, "I'm not feeling it right now. But if you send me a musician, a psalmic minstrel, the atmosphere will shift, and I will be able to hear from the Lord."

That is the psalmist's anointing. It's the power that is in you to break open atmospheres in which signs and wonders and miracles can occur. When the musician played, Elisha was able to hear the voice of the Lord. The power of God was released through an anointed worshiper and everything shifted. Elisha was able to give divine instructions by revelation that occurred in an atmosphere of worship. The psalmist changed everything. Even the prophet was unable to hear God until the psalmist broke open the heavenly realm.

Another biblical example of the psalmist's anointing is found in a familiar passage from First Samuel 16. Samuel was searching for the next man who God wanted to anoint as king over Israel. God directed him that he would find the next king among Jesse's sons. Samuel found Jesse and looked at his sons from the oldest to the youngest. Son after son after son, Samuel did not see one who God said was chosen to be king. "Are these all of your sons?" Samuel asked.

"The youngest one is still out with the sheep." Jesse hadn't bothered to call David in because David was the least likely to be brought to Samuel's attention. David had grown up with the sheep, and he spent all his hours in the field with God, alone with the sheep. That's where he learned worship, and that's where he developed his skills as a musician.

Samuel asked for David to be brought in, and immediately Samuel heard from the Lord that David was to be king. Samuel took a horn full of oil and poured it over David's head, anointing him as the future king. David received the anointing at that time, and verse 13 tells us that "the Spirit of the Lord came upon David from that day forward."

The Spirit of the Lord was on David, but King Saul was not so fortunate. The Spirit of the Lord departed from him, and he was tormented by a distressing spirit. His servants were concerned for him and they offered to "seek out a man who is a skillful player on the harp. And it shall be that he will play it with his hand when the distressing spirit from God is upon you, and you shall be well" (1 Samuel 16:16).

Remember *zamar?* That is the power of the anointing. The worshiper has the ability to break oppression off of people and open the doors for God's blessing. Also, notice that David was described as a "skillful" musician. Anointing and skill go hand in hand. If you don't develop your craft, your anointing will be capped off. If you want to go to another level in the anointing, grow in your musicianship. That only happens through practice, which I will address later.

David carried that psalmist's anointing. He had been anointed with oil by Samuel, but he had honed his musical skills and fostered that intimacy with God long before, while he was out in the pastures with the sheep. It was forged through encounter and time spent in God's presence. He refined his gift through nearness with God. Like David, we can also grow in the anointing by doing one simple task: draw closer. Draw near to Him and He will draw near to you.

LOVE AND FAVOR

One of Saul's servants knew that David was a musician. He told Saul, "There is a son of Jesse who is a skillful player. He's a mighty man of valor and a man of war. He's handsome and articulate, and the Lord is with him." So Saul sent for David.

David found so much favor with Saul that he became Saul's armor bearer, his most trusted servant. Saul requested of Jesse that David be allowed to stay with him because he valued his company so much. Whenever David was with Saul, the tormenting spirit would leave Saul. Whenever the spirit returned, David would play his worship in Saul's presence, and Saul would be refreshed and healed.

The passage also points out that David loved Saul greatly. David didn't scorn Saul for his affliction and struggles. Rather, he looked upon Saul with compassion. He could have been haughty or condescending because God's pleasure had been removed from Saul and placed upon David. He could have been arrogant or flaunted that God had anointed him as the next king. Instead, David was moved with compassion for Saul and was stirred with love for him, despite all of Saul's wickedness. Saul was least deserving of love, yet David gave it freely.

I believe that demonstration of love bubbled forth from David's intimacy with God as well. We are unable to love others well until we have experienced God's love. That kind of intimacy only comes through time dwelling in God's presence and sowing into worship. It's part of the splat factor. When we spend time drawing near to God, He gifts us with the ability to love the unlovable people.

Not only did David's love touch Saul's heart, his worship healed Saul's spirit. David's music, played skillfully on a harp, carried the anointing to deliver Saul from a tormenting spirit. The psalmist's anointing carries power over demons. We can cast out evil spirits with our worship. We don't have to shout them out or ask their names or anything like that. We can simply play them out, sing them out, cast them out! As you play your instruments and simply devote your heart to God, people around you will experience deliverance. There is power in the anointing—power for deliverance and healing and breakthrough. It's a power gained by spending time in the secret place. The anointing is birthed in intimacy and relationship with God.

ALL ARE ANOINTED

We all carry the psalmist's anointing. When it seems that one person carries more anointing than others, it is not because there was a different degree or measure of anointing given to that person. David was anointed just like Saul had been anointed. Yet, they experienced the anointing differently. There are three reasons why some people seem to have more anointing than others.

First, anointing is connected to intimacy with God. That was the difference between David and Saul. Saul had rejected God while David's life was marked by constant interaction and encounter with God. He spent time in that secret place. He knew God and God knew him. The anointing flourished under the fertile ground of intimacy with God.

A second reason that anointing can seem greater in some people is because anointing can be grown. The anointing increases when we work the anointing given to us. Some people don't do anything with the anointing they have already been given. They never posture themselves in such a way to minister unto God and others to release the anointing in them. They just sit with it. It's similar to Jesus' parable about the talents. Those who do nothing with the gifts God gives them will lose what they have, and others who run with the anointing will be given more. The determining factor in the fruitfulness of the anointing is how well the person has cultivated the measure of anointing they were given. The seemingly most anointed people are the ones who have worked at it, and the anointing has grown as a result of their faithfulness.

The third reason some people seem to have more anointing than others is related to how we apply the anointing. We must identify the context and giftings in which our anointing best flows through us. We all have the same anointing in Jesus, but we are called to different functions. If we are operating in the wrong function, the expression of the anointing will be limited. But if we operate in the giftings and callings God has placed on our lives, we flow more powerfully in the anointing.

For example, everyone is called to worship, but not everyone is called to lead worship. We all have anointing because the Anointed One lives in each of us. However, the psalmist's anointing rests on those who are called and purposed by God to be psalmists. If you aren't functioning in the right calling, your anointing will get you somewhere, but you can only go so far. If you feel frustrated in a certain function you are performing, it may be because you weren't called to that function. There may be other reasons for that frustration as well, but one possible reason is you don't understand your calling.

It is important that we understand our calling according to His purpose. Romans 8:28 tells us that "All things work together for good to those who love God, to those who are called according to His purpose." We have a calling that is according to His purpose. As we draw near to Him, He speaks to us about that. He draws it out of us, and the purpose grows out of relationship with Him. You will have maximum impact in the anointing when you are operating in your purpose.

One time a gentleman joined our choir who could not sing at all. He loved God with all his heart, and he was an excellent servant. He would have done anything for me. I loved him, and he loved me. He was always the first one to arrive at rehearsals and the last one to leave. He would give and serve in any way he could find. But he couldn't hold a pitch with a fork. He wasn't functioning in his calling.

I loved him, but he was making worship leading difficult for me. Not only could he not sing, but the people around him couldn't sing either because he would throw them off key. They couldn't hear the music correctly if near him. Nobody wanted to sit by him because he was so tone deaf. As much as I loved the guy, we had a real problem. But I wasn't sure how to address it.

One day he approached me with a smile. "Hey Steve, check out these pictures." He handed me some photographs. They were absolutely beautiful. Stunning landscapes shot with artful contrast. Perfectly framed portraits with beautiful focus and dimension.

"Where did you get these?" I asked.

"I shot them," he replied. "What do you think?"

"Oh my goodness! These are spectacular!"

Then it struck me. This man was operating in the wrong calling! "You know what? I think you should really pursue photography. You are anointed for this. Power comes through your eyes and into the photographs. I sense a calling on your life for this. You don't belong in the bass section of the choir. You were made to be a photographer."

The man listened to my advice and began putting his efforts to developing his skills and growing the anointing in the arena of photography. Today he is tremendously successful. His pictures are in magazines and he holds a position as a staff photographer.

When he was in the choir, he was functioning in an anointing that he wasn't called to be in. He enjoyed it, and that took him so far. But he was limited in what he could succeed in. And, frankly, he was limiting the rest of us on the team as well. When he moved into God's intended purpose, he flourished. The anointing came upon him in that function of photography, and God is using him tremendously in that capacity to bring glory to Him. He may not have a psalmist's anointing, but he definitely has a photographer's anointing.

We don't all have to be singers or musicians. But we are all called to be worshipers and to function in the unique role God has for us. When we submit to God's calling and we live obedient to His will, we stay on the track He set before us. When we function in the role God called us to, His purposes can be accomplished and accelerated in and through us.

CHAPTER 7

GROWING IN THE ANOINTING

My dad was my hero. He took me in as his own son when he married my mom. He served God faithfully his entire life. I saw him sow into God's presence day after day. The overflow of his relationship with God became the fertile ground upon which the people in our little church flourished. He modeled something I hope to be able to emulate in my life—he was committed to the calling God set before him every day of his life. He never once decided it was time to take a break from God's path of destiny. When he was 97 years old, he finally decided it was time to close down the church. The reason wasn't because he stopped wanting to follow God in his calling. It was much more practical than that. He and my mom had simply outlived their entire congregation.

They had been the only two left in the church for some time. Yet my 97-year-old dad would still wake up every Sunday morning and dress his 97-year-old body in a perfectly pressed suit and a sharp tie from his collection he'd had for decades. He'd prepare a beautiful sermon and preach as if proclaiming to a crowd of hundreds. He would deliver his sermon with as much gumption as his aging frame could muster, and Mom would play the piano while they both worshiped in their living room. Every Sunday he performed this act of devotion until it was just too hard for him to continue. He died a couple years later. Dad's last words were, "We serve a mighty God. We serve a living God." I pray I finish as well.

Dad knew something. God had anointed him to preach the gospel, and Dad had been faithful to grow that anointing. He sought after God and refined his technique. He studied and learned from others. He was voracious for God's presence and guidance as he sought to grow in the anointing.

Each of us is anointed because we are the temples who house the Anointed One. However, not all of us will fulfill all that is in God's heart for us to do. He has a destiny and a plan. It's a plan for our lives that is woven into His redemptive plan of human history. We all have a calling, a destiny to fulfill. We won't live out that destiny by anointing alone. We must seek His presence, be obedient to follow His leadership, and grow in the measure of anointing given to us.

Remember when David was anointed by Samuel to be the next king of Israel in First Samuel 16? The passage states that at the time David was anointed, the Spirit of the Lord came upon him from that day forward. But David didn't become king that day. He wasn't ready yet. He already had the anointing, but he wasn't yet ready to rule. The anointing had yet to be refined and developed. It was grown through relationship with God, His Word, and through tests and trials. Our anointing grows as our character is developed. The ups and downs of life can be crises that force us to press in to faith and build our character.

David still had to develop a character and relationship with God that was strong enough to hold the weight of the kingship. He had the anointing, but he had to grow into the man who could carry the destiny.

FOUR GROWTH FACTORS

David was able to increase God's presence on his life. I believe there are four factors that David understood that helped him grow in the anointing: 1) hunger for God, 2) a worshiping heart, 3) intimacy with God, and 4) enjoyment of God.

The first key David understood was *hunger.* David was hungry for God's presence. His hunger was illustrated poignantly in Psalm 63:1-8:

> *O God, You are my God;*
> *Early will I seek You;*
> *My soul thirsts for You;*
> *My flesh longs for You*
> *In a dry and thirsty land*

Where there is no water.
So I have looked for You in the sanctuary,
To see Your power and Your glory.
Because Your lovingkindness is better than life,
My lips shall praise You.
Thus I will bless You while I live;
I will lift up my hands in Your name.
My soul shall be satisfied as
with marrow and fatness,
And my mouth shall praise You with joyful lips.
When I remember You on my bed,
I meditate on You in the night watches.
Because You have been my help,
Therefore in the shadow of Your wings
I will rejoice.
My soul follows close behind You;
Your right hand upholds me.

This psalm expresses David's innate, driving hunger for more of the Lord. The anointing develops under longing. A gnawing longing urges us to reach into God's anointing and pull it in. We become so hungry for God's presence that we push aside all earthly attachments and just seek Him. We long for His presence.

Psalm 84 also shows this longing: "How lovely is your dwelling place, O Lord of hosts! My soul longs, yes, faints for the courts of the Lord; my heart and flesh sing for joy to the living God" (Psalm 84:1-2 ESV). I love David's imagery in this passage. My whole being thrills with joy at His name. It reminds me of when my children were small. I'd come home and open the door, and their faces would beam with excitement. That should be our disposition toward God. Just the mention of His name should cause us to light up with delight and joy.

David knew how to worship God like that. I want to have that kind of worshiper's heart—the kind that longs to see Daddy's face again. When we experience that kind of hunger for God, just the mention of His name elicits total elation. David's hunger was the driving force behind his worship. Hunger wrongly handled can turn inward and become fruitless. We must follow David's example and translate our hunger into worship.

Worship is the second key for increasing God's presence. David knew how to worship; in fact, he set the standard high in regard to worship. He worshiped ravenously and with abandon. When he realized he had stopped worshiping, he would tell himself to worship more: "Bless the Lord, O my soul; and all that is within me, bless His holy name!" (Psalm 103:1). We can speak to our soul and our flesh. When our flesh isn't aligning with God's purposes, we can command our soul and flesh to come in line with our spirit to worship.

The third key David used to increase God's presence was *intimacy* with God. Intimacy means we come close to God and love on Him. In that close place, we know God, and we are known by God. It's the environment of vulnerability in which love flourishes. Intimacy heals the soul.

David knew God. He had many experiences with Him, and David had come to know God's character through experience. In Psalm 103 and 91 David declares, "For as the heavens are high above the earth, so great is His mercy toward them who fear Him. He who dwells in the secret place of the Most High shall abide under the shadow of the Almighty. I will say of the Lord, 'He is my refuge and my fortress; My God, in Him I will trust.'"

The reason David could state, God is my refuge, my fortress, and my God, is because David had been through challenging struggles. He had fought for his life. He needed a refuge and a fortress, and God was faithful to provide for him. He had personal experience with the great mercy toward those who fear God.

Not only did David know God, but God knew David. Psalm 139:1-10 says:

> *O lord, thou hast searched me, and known me. Thou knowest my downsitting and mine uprising, thou understandest my thought afar off. Thou compassest my path and my lying down, and art acquainted with all my ways. For there is not a word in my tongue, but, lo, O Lord, thou knowest it altogether. Thou hast beset me behind and before, and laid thine hand upon me. Such knowledge is too wonderful for me; it is high, I cannot attain unto it. Whither shall I go from thy spirit? or whither shall I flee from thy presence? If I ascend up into heaven, thou art there: if I make my bed in hell, behold, thou art there. If I take the wings of the morning, and dwell in the uttermost*

parts of the sea; even there shall thy hand lead me, and thy right hand shall hold me (KJV).

David knew God and was known by God. Love flourishes in intimacy. Psalm 91:14-16 tells us God's thoughts about David:

Because he has set his love upon Me, therefore I will deliver him. I will set him on high because he has known My name. He shall call upon Me, and I will answer him. I will be with him in trouble; I will deliver him and honor him. With long life will I satisfy him, and show him My salvation.

They knew each other, and because of that love, God says that He will honor David. In the place of intimacy, God meets all our needs, and He honors us. When God honors us, it releases us to be who we were created to be. In effect God is saying, "I acknowledge the gift in you, so be more of who you are." That allows us to function in what we are called to function in. He releases us from all the hindrances preventing us from becoming what we are called to become.

The key to that passage is "because he [David] has set his love upon Me." When you set your love upon the Lord, it invokes a response from Him. He is moved by your love. As you draw near to Him, He promises to draw near to you. That is intimacy. When you love on Him, He loves on you back.

Through all the trials, challenges, emotional ups and down, and intimacy with God, David is converged into his destiny as king. He honed the anointing he had received as a youth. The meandering path took David through many obstacles, but David did eventually become king. We, too, grow into our anointing and calling as we focus on developing our intimate relationship with God.

The fourth key to growing in the anointing is to *enjoy God.* When you have intimacy with God, He becomes your Source for joy. A relationship with God requires encounters and exchanges. He meets us, and we are ruined for anything but finding our joy in Him.

I've been to churches where it looks like no one is having fun. No one seems to enjoy anything. They especially don't know how to enjoy God. It seems a little maniacal to me. They sing, "Oh Happy Day," but there are no smiles! They seem to receive equal enjoyment from announcements and worship. That doesn't make sense to me.

When I first applied for the job at the organ church in Portland, I had my first interaction with joyless church people, and it baffled me. I had completed my first interview with the pastor, and I was asked to lead worship one Sunday to try out for the position. "We have to get the approval of the council," he explained. They wanted to see me lead worship before they hired me. I had never heard of a church council. I grew up in Mom and Dad's church. I was used to Dad preaching for three and a half hours before Auntie Alma would start dancing around the room. We could only seat seventy people, but it rarely got that full. I had no idea what a council was or what it did.

"What's the council?" I asked the pastor.

"The church council is run by the board." Well, that clarified the situation perfectly!

So I showed up on Sunday really nervous. It was a big church and this was my one and only chance to impress the mysterious council. I had carefully selected the songs, and I had my music all together. I sat down to the piano and began. Halfway through the first song, about twelve people on each side walked solemnly down the aisle. They were dressed completely in black, and they walked with a rigidity that made me shudder. They sat down with furrowed brows. No hint of a smile anywhere. A couple of them looked over their bulletins. *This must be the council,* I thought to myself. *They are here to judge me!*

I continued leading worship, and I tried to appear composed. The men dressed in black kept looking down or absently reading the bulletin. *They hate me! This is it—there's no way I'm getting this job. Well, Lord, Your will be done.*

I was told before the service that at the end of worship, communion would be served. I didn't know much about how that worked because that hadn't been part of Mom and Dad's church. Finally, I was done with the worship set audition, and it was time for communion. All of a sudden, the men in black stood simultaneously and walked to the communion table. They began to serve communion to the people. This wasn't the council. These were the communion people! I did eventually get the job, but I never forgot the depressing communion men in black.

I love joy! It's a major theme for me, and I sing about it a lot. If we have joy, our faces should show it. I have also learned that you can't always judge a person by the way he or she looks. I was in a service once in the Netherlands, and there was an older man sitting right on the front row with the worst look on his face. I had to try to block him out as I worshiped so I could focus. I thought either this guy really hated me or he didn't understand a word of English. I wondered why he didn't just get up and leave because he looked miserable sitting there. After the service, he darted up to me and spoke in flawless English, "That was the most amazing service I have ever been in," he declared. I was speechless, but I was thinking, *Dude, why don't you let your face show it next time!* We look at the outward appearance, but God looks at the heart.

Joy is a natural outflow of relationship with God; and as we enjoy God, we develop the anointing that is on our lives. Our worship releases His abiding presence developed through intimacy. As we grow in that anointing, everything changes. Like David, we move from the sheep's pasture to the throne. Growth is the connection point between our anointing and our destiny.

THE SECRET PLACE OF GROWTH

Growth doesn't happen overnight. It is nurtured day after day and year to year. We have to sow into the anointing to see growth. We can sow into that anointing when nobody else is around. The growth happens in the secret place. When you sit down to worship, and it's just you and

God and no one else, that's when you are pouring into yourself. You tell yourself and God, I'm going to worship regardless what anyone else does. I'm going to do it because He's worthy and I can't survive without Him. As we pour our worship out on God like Mary's alabaster jar, He also pours back into us. It becomes a place of overflow, and that overflow produces the growth.

It's easy for me to go into a meeting and start worshiping because I've already been worshiping all day long. I don't just start worshiping when I get on the *altar*. The *altar* is the overflow. The *altar* is where we pour out all that God has poured into us in the secret place. When you sow into the secret place, you never have to prepare yourself for worship. Your life has become worship, and all you do is overflow. You're always prepared because you've sown into the anointing. Ministering out of the overflow is what keeps you from burning out. The anointing is referred to as oil on many occasions. If your lamp is not full of oil, you're burning the wick and sooner or later the wick will be consumed, and there will be nothing left to burn. I've seen it happen; that is why it's so important to sow into your anointing, so your lamp is always full of fresh oil!

God is searching for a resting place for His presence. He wants to make His home in us, but it requires us to take the time to worship Him. When we are gathered together in worship, He comes as we establish a throne for Him on our praises.

There's a distinction between God's omnipresence and His manifest presence. God is always everywhere, so there's no place that is absent of God's presence. But that's not the kind of presence I'm referring to when I talk about His presence coming in worship and being enthroned on our praises. The distinction is in whether or not we acknowledge His presence. When we acknowledge Him in praise, we make a place for His presence to be made known to us in the midst of our meeting. It's a presence we can feel and detect with our senses, not just through faith. There are many ways to acknowledge God's presence, and different streams or denominations do this differently. The method is not important as long as we acknowledge God's presence in our worship and make a place for His presence to be made known to us.

The tabernacle in the Old Testament was the tent of praise. Tabernacle imagery is used throughout the Bible as a symbol for the place where God's presence dwelled. In the New Covenant, our life and our worship become the tabernacle which form a habitation for God's presence.

In Acts 15:15-17, James reminded the others of a prophecy from God stating, "I will return and will rebuild the tabernacle of David, which has fallen down; I will rebuild its ruins, and I will set it up; so that the rest of mankind may seek the Lord, even all the Gentiles." God is rebuilding His tabernacle of praise. When we worship, we are building a habitation in which He can enter and rest.

I was once in a meeting in which God gave us a picture of us pulling on the ropes that heft up a large tent. That's what praise does. When we worship, we pull the ropes to erect a habitation in which God's presence can come and dwell.

There are times when I'm leading worship and it feels like I'm coming up against a wall. My first reaction is to escalate the worship to push through that in order to take people deeper into worship. The problem is that they may not be ready for that. Also, pushing through can be making something happen in the flesh. I don't want to use my musical muscle to plow my way into God's presence. It doesn't work that way. Often the best thing to do in those situations is to pull back. I pull back and bring it back to simple thanksgiving and praise. I remind the people who God is, and we spend time just praising God for His mighty deeds and His attributes. We dial down the frenzy and come back to center—praise God for His attributes. Pull on the ropes of the tent. Maturity in the anointing doesn't always mean doing more. Maturity sometimes means we are strong enough to do less.

God loves to encounter us in corporate worship, but He is also looking for individuals who will be a tabernacle of praise. His eyes are looking to and fro for hearts that are fully His. He's searching for a dwelling place where His glory can rest. Our goal as worshipers is to create an environment that becomes a suitable place for God. A suitable habitation is a heart fully abandoned to Him. It's a throne of worship on a sacrificed life.

When God's presence comes, we surrender completely to Him. He is enthroned on our praise. A throne is a place from which a king rules. When God is enthroned in our praise, He takes His place as King and His will is done. He takes charge.

WHAT'S NEXT?

Sometimes when God is enthroned and takes charge, it messes up our plans. I've been in many meetings when the glory of the Lord comes and the whole agenda had to be abandoned so that we could seek His face. Sometimes He messes things up so much that we are uncertain what we should do next. What we had on the agenda doesn't seem appropriate, but we aren't sure what is appropriate. It's definitely not time to move on to announcements or offering. But what do we do? I love that!

It feels a little scary to not know what to do next, but those are also the moments that we know God is having His way. It's the best situation to be in. Our nature is to stick to the original plan, but it's best to just abandon all expectation and acknowledge the whole reason for the agenda was to hopefully encounter God. Now that He has come, we don't need the agenda.

Sometimes, we can inadvertently misunderstand what God is doing. His presence comes, and we're not sure if we should worship more or minister healing or something else entirely. Occasionally we will misunderstand and zig when God goes zag. Give yourself grace in those situations because the pressure is not on us. His ways are higher than ours, and if He has something He really wants to do, He will make that clear. If it's unclear, pick a direction to go in and just enjoy His presence with you.

Sometimes we need to just stop everything. I was once in a meeting in Alabama when God's presence came in the room and He said to me, "Stop."

"Stop? We're in the middle of a song, God."

"Stop what you're doing."

So I stopped, right in the middle of a really loud and frenzied song. Silence. The people were a little confused, but only for a moment because then God's glory came in to a much greater level. It felt like God walked into the room, and every person was absolutely silent. For forty-five minutes, the entire room was absolutely silent. People were trembling as we were all completely aware of God's tangible presence. A guest speaker was scheduled to minister, but he never made it to the pulpit. We all just waited in silence on God. No laughing, no shouting, no singing just a whole lot of vibrating in His glory. We let God mess up all our plans, and His presence was thick in the silence.

Eventually someone began to shout from the back. When he did, the Spirit of God fell on the guest speaker, and he ran around the whole sanctuary six or seven times in a Holy Ghost sprint shouting all the way. He sprinted round and round till he bounded up to the platform and fell flat on his face. *He won't be speaking tonight,* I thought to myself.

God really likes to mess things up. We need to stop trying to make sense of it and just agree that if God wants a mess, then we just want to get messy with Him. I love the wrecking ball of the Spirit of God, the weight of His glory, tangible, undeniable…glorious!

THE KEY—FLEXIBILITY

The key to growing in the anointing is being willing to follow God's lead. It requires flexibility. Be flexible to be led. We tend to like routine. We want to do the same things over and over. Sometimes that structure is good, but at other times "structure" is the word we use to mask the fact that we are stuck in a rut. When we become inflexible, it stops the flow of the Holy Spirit from our meetings. If He's not allowed to mess things up when He comes, He probably won't come.

One definition of insanity is doing the same thing over and over again and expecting a different result. Our meetings sometimes look a lot like insanity. We get stuck in our rut of doing things the same way and wanting God to move, but He doesn't, because there's no room to move. He doesn't have the freedom to do what He wants to do. What do we expect? For God to breathe on a program or agenda that we have been using, yet God hasn't breathed on it for a long time? It may be time to abandon that plan. Flexibility is a key because God is spontaneous. Don't let your ruts or traditions prevent you from experiencing the move of God.

The Israelites had to depend on God to lead them through the wilderness. Exodus 13:21 describes how the glory of God directed them: "And the Lord went before them by day in a pillar of cloud to lead the way, and by night in a pillar of fire to give them light." God's glory still comes down to direct us and lead us. Sometimes He goes in a direction different from what we expect or want. It doesn't matter because we just need to be with Him. The reason we follow His lead is because we want to be with Him. He is our light, and we end up in the shadows if we don't follow Him.

We also follow Him because He wants to take us somewhere. He is directing us. There's something He's trying to accomplish. This is the divine encounter through worship—expect it, anticipate it, God wants to meet with us as much as we want to meet with Him. An example of this is seen in Numbers 11:25: "The Lord came down in the cloud, and spoke to him, and took of the Spirit that was upon him, and placed the same upon the seventy elders; and it happened, when the Spirit rested upon them, that they prophesied, although they never did so again." The glory came on them because God wanted to speak. He came upon them and the seventy elders prophesied. Likewise, sometimes God shows up in our meetings because He wants to do something specific. We have to be willing to be led so we can do what He wants to do. That's all part of the divine encounter. It may be prophecy, healing, deliverance, repentance, or many other things. We have to remain open to God's agenda when the glory comes.

GLORY POWER

Finally, the glory of God comes at times simply to bring His weighty presence. That kind of glory is *kavod* glory, and it means weight. It presses down and we feel smaller and smaller as His weight overwhelms us. It evokes reverence in us. Second Chronicles 5:11-14 gives us an example of the *kavod* glory. This scene takes place upon the completion and dedication of Solomon's temple. The priests had just carried the Ark of the Covenant into the Holy of Holies.

> *And it came to pass when the priests came out of the Most Holy Place (for all the priests who were present had sanctified themselves, without keeping to their divisions), and the Levites who were the singers, all those of Asaph and Heman and Jeduthun, with their sons and their brethren, stood at the east end of the altar, clothed in white linen, having cymbals, stringed instruments and harps, and with them one hundred and twenty priests sounding with trumpets—indeed it came to pass, when the trumpeters and singers were as one, to make one sound to be heard in praising and thanking the Lord, and when they lifted up their voice with the trumpets and cymbals and instruments of music, and praised the Lord, saying: "For He is good, for His mercy endures forever," that the house, the house of the Lord, was filled with a cloud, so that the priests could not continue ministering because of the cloud; for the glory of the Lord filled the house of God.*

Before I discuss the weighty glory on the priests, let me take a moment to point out how beautiful it is that the priests had set aside all their divisions. They disregarded any disagreements and chose to be single-minded about entering the Holy Place and placing the Ark. They agreed that they were going into God's presence together. I find that remarkable. As worship leaders, pastors, and people with varied giftings and callings, we must choose to put those divisions aside for the purpose of entering into God's presence together.

There is such power in the corporate agreement. All the ministers were in one spirit. Then the house was filled with a cloud of glory *(kavod)* so weighty that they could not even continue ministering. The cloud of His presence overwhelmed them. Many times God will show up, and we are simply overwhelmed. That's the glory! It's who He is, what He does—it's every part of Him invading our circumstances and bringing us in to a heavenly realm of His very existence.

The overwhelming *kavod* glory presence invokes a reverential fear. Psalm 40:3 says, "many will see it and fear, and will trust in the Lord." When His glory comes and we are in awe, we often don't know what to do. That is the fear of the Lord. It's not a fear that makes us afraid. It's a fear that puts a reverence on His presence and recognition that we are so much less than God and He is our dependence.

I believe we will see more and more of the *kavod* glory in our meetings. It's the glory that leaves us speechless and in awe. Like the priests who were overwhelmed in the glory cloud, we will be completely unable to perform our normal functions. The preachers won't be able to preach. The prophets won't be able to prophesy. The musicians won't be able to play. We will be filled with reverential fear, and we will only be able to awe. It's not so much a cloud or a pillar of fire that awes us as it is Him! Although that would be pretty amazing, I just want Him. Raw God, all that He is in His beauty—and all we can do is cast our crowns before Him. I think I'd like that.

CHAPTER 8

WORSHIP DYNAMICS

The Sunday decades ago when I tried out for the worship position at the large Portland church was the beginning of a journey for me. I had no idea God had such a crazy adventure in mind when I took the first baby steps down this path of destiny. Since those early days, I've had the opportunity to lead for crowds of two and crowds of thousands. I've traveled the world and I've recorded albums. I've made a lot of mistakes along the way, and I've learned a few things in the process.

Worship leading is an art. Like any art, there are certain tools and techniques we can learn to help us develop our craft. This chapter focuses on some of the more technical aspects of worship leading, and I hope some of my experience will make your learning process a little easier.

Before you begin, you need to identify how to plan your worship set. This is determined by the structure of the service in which you are leading worship.

In the first scenario, the services are structured and scheduled. Many local churches follow this model for their Sunday morning services. There is an allotted amount of time for worship, and that's it before they move on to the next event in the service. You may only have fifteen minutes. If so, make it the best fifteen minutes of their week. Go for it in fifteen minutes. To be honest with you, I used to think, *Fifteen minutes? I can't get anything done in 15 minutes!* It seemed like a throw-away kind of thing, a preliminary to the main event. Our worship is the main event! It's Him, it will always be Him.

When I realized it's not about me and my perfectly planned worship set, it really freed me up to be joyful in my approach to fifteen minutes. *You mean I get to lead a bunch of people into God's presence? What a privilege! Okay then, this will be God's fifteen minutes of fame in our little world!* I like to joke that I can get people in with fifteen minutes—I just don't know if I can get them back out. I've seen it happen; it doesn't take long for God to show up because He's already there, and if you're ministering out of the overflow, it's already going on, you're just joining Heaven's symphony. You never know, I've seen fifteen minutes turn into two and a half hours! Be ready for anything!

A second scenario has structure but with flexibility. There are few time constraints. This allows you to spend more time in worship, but if worship doesn't seem to be progressing, then you move on to other things. This type of structure might happen in healing meetings or prophetic meetings.

A third model has no time constraint in worship. There's no agenda other than to worship. Prayer rooms often use this model. Worship is the sole goal and only factor in determining the flow of these sessions.

Which of these models is right? Which is best? None of them. They are all useful in different contexts. We are priests who are called first to serve. As worship leaders, of course we the want liberty to let it rip. We would like to always have a prophetic worship team with no time or space restrictions. But we need to be prepared for whatever task we are asked to serve in. We should be prepared to do it all. If it's only fifteen minutes, lead the people into God's presence in fifteen minutes. It shouldn't be difficult for you to enter into worship because you should have been worshiping for the twenty-three hours and forty-five minutes before that.

THE FRAMING MODEL

I've developed a model for planning worship sets that works in any service format. It works just as well for fifteen minutes as well as 24-7 worship. I call it the framing model.

The first step in the framing model is to *identify through the Holy Spirit a focal point*. The focal point is the main purpose God wants to communicate in the worship set. Examples of a focal point may be: the Holy Spirit, intimacy with God, or the sweet presence of Jesus. The focal point can be determined by the Holy Spirit, leadership, or the flow of the meeting. When we are preparing for a worship set and we pray, I always ask the Holy Spirit to determine the focal point. Asking, "What's on Your heart, God," He tells us what He wants us to focus on in worship. Sometimes the pastor or leader in charge of the service has a sense of what God wants to do, and we should use that topic as our focus for our worship set. Other times we let the flow of the meeting determine the focus.

With framing we also have the freedom to adjust our focus. We may have started out with one focus, but then maybe the flow of the worship goes into a whole new direction. Have you ever seen birds sitting all lined up on an electrical wire? All of a sudden they all launch at the same time and at first it seems like chaos, but all of a sudden, they all come into agreement with the leader and follow in a beautiful dance with the wind. Once the leader catches the shift in the wind, they all move in unison to a different direction. That's how we adjust our focus as we need to. Always be ready for your plans to be hijacked by the flow of the Spirit. The key is to make sure you have a focal point to begin with. The Holy Spirit will give you a launching pad, and from there you can move with the wind as it ebbs and flows.

The second step in the framing model is to *frame the set*. A frame keeps the focus on the focal point. A frame around a piece of art enhances the art, but everything on the frame points to the focal point. We frame when we select songs that support our focal point. We determine directions to move in worship and the prophetic that keep the focus in mind. Like the focal point, the frame has to be flexible as well. You may have to *reframe* and change directions during a service. Build your set with a goal and purpose in mind and let everything lead to that point, but be flexible.

The frame is meant to draw your eye to the picture, not the frame. The content is important, not the frame. Likewise, we have to remain aware that the focal point is more important than the music pointing to the focal point. We can have a beautiful frame—the music—but the frame has failed to do its job if the people only notice the frame. We should be masterful musicians, but our music should never get in the way of what God wants to do.

This model works for any time setting. Even if your time is very restricted, a Holy Spirit-led worship service can be very powerful. Don't allow a time restraint to determine how you feel or how you respond. After all, it's not about you or the way you feel. It's not a stage, it's not a platform—it's an altar. We submit ourselves as a sacrifice on the altar. We can show the focal point in five minutes or five hours, so it's not about the time.

A key to the framing model is *flexibility*. The main way we gain flexibility is through a well-rounded repertoire of music. You should develop a storehouse of songs that you always have available to you that you can access at any time. Become a voice or an oracle of the Holy Spirit, so if the Spirit says to adjust the focal point or the frame, you are always ready. Have a collection of songs prepared that cover a wide array of topics so that you are prepared for any contingency. It also gives you ease of mind. When you know that you have a plethora of songs at your disposal, there is less stress on you to come up with something brilliant on the spot.

Current songs are great because they are new and everyone likes to sing the latest releases if they are accessible. However, keep a catalog of older standards available because they give you the flexibility you need for the framing model. They may not be the latest songs, but they are songs that everyone knows, so it will be easy for the people to follow you when you change directions.

The bottom line is *engagement*, there is so much power in the corporate agreement. Remember the priests in one accord? That is the goal. The commanded blessing comes in unity. Don't settle for half agreement, three-quarters agreement. If we can get everyone on the same page, and there is unity in the room, anything can happen. You as a leader have to know the people you are serving by leading them into the presence of God.

Every church has a demographic. As worship leaders we need to be aware of the demographic of the house. You can stretch the envelope into different styles, but only so far. Remain true to where you are serving and what the vision of the church is. Anything you try to force on your people that is not what they are ready for will turn into division. The enemy can use worship to divide and conquer. I only say this through experience. If you try to force your musical preference on a church that is not ready for your preference,

I can almost guarantee that you won't have a staff position too long; unless of course, you are in agreement with the pastor's vision. Be gentle my friend.

Communicate with your pastor. It may take a while, to bring the people forward. That's okay. Between the pastor and you, in open dialog, you can steer the ship. The worst thing you can do as a staff worship leader is to alienate your people. Your preference may not be God's for that house, place, and time. Be flexible my friend, God will have His way—eventually—when we get out of His way.

Have you ever looked at the back of a hymnal? There is usually a topical index that lists all the songs by category. So if you want to find a hymn on salvation, you just have to look under that heading and you find all the songs in the hymnal relating to salvation. I highly recommend you develop the same type of system for your worship repertoire. Whether you have paper music or digital versions, find a way to catalog all your songs by topic. That way, if you sense the Holy Spirit say to move your focal point to evangelism, it will only take you a moment to reframe a whole set to that topic.

Another key to the framing model is *developing trust with your leader.* You need to talk with your pastor regularly about what he or she envisions in worship and where you want to work together to take the congregation. You need to be able to trust the pastor, and the pastor needs to be able to trust you. If the pastor comes to the front with an exhortation or prophetic picture, you have to trust the Spirit moving through him or her and respond with your music accordingly. When you trust each other, you can build upon each other and together take the people to a higher place. You may have been planning to go a different direction, but you need to submit and follow what the Spirit is saying through leadership.

To be a good musician, you also need to be able to flow in any style at any time. Don't corner yourself into one style or genre of music. I love to incorporate jazz and classical into my music. There are some genres I enjoy more than others, but I try to be prepared to play any of them. A diversity of styles is part of the hallmark of a good musician, and it's another tool that gives you greater flexibility.

It may seem obvious (but it's often overlooked), but a key to being a flexible musician is practice. You have to be good at your instrument to be flexible. You have to refine the skills of changing styles, genres, keys, and rhythms at a moment's notice. Practice your instrument until you become fluent. When you are fluent in a language, you don't have to think about what words you use. The words you want flow out of your mouth without cognizant choices and decisions. Practice your instrument until you reach that point of fluency where you don't have to think about chord changes or progressions or rhythms. Then practice some more! Sunday morning once a week is not enough time spent at your instrument to become fluent.

Worship leading is not a hobby—it is a lifestyle. People in weekend garage bands have a hobby. If you are called to worship then it is your life. So what importance do you place on your life? How important is His life in you?

I understand how difficult it is for leaders to find good musicians. Raising up good musicians is one of my mandates as a father and mentor in the worship field. Listen, I know what it's like to find anyone breathing to be on the worship team. "Oh you play drums?" "Can you play next Sunday?" It's about making disciples, not hiring muzos. So what if the person can't keep too much of a beat? Is he or she trainable, flexible? Are you skilled enough to help him or her grow? That's biblical according to Ephesians—we are called to equip and to train the fellowship of believers.

I believe the best musicians should be in the church, returning to God what He has freely gifted us with. So as a church we need to raise the standard of musicianship, or otherwise we will miss the prodigals who are looking for somewhere to plug in. We need fathers, mentors, teachers who can train and equip the Levites in worship and fluency on their instruments. We need musicians who are sold out on God, and will practice their craft to become the skilled psalmic minstrels I previously spoke about. These are the ones who carry the power and the presence of God on their instruments. It's happening, albeit ever so slowly.

Remember G, G, G, C, C, C? Well if you haven't heard what's going on at the International House of Prayer (IHOP), I encourage you to plug into that. They've gone from two chords to masterful musicianship. How did that happen? They set up an academy of musicianship—training for musicians and singers (who by the way I categorize equally in this title) so they can excel on their instruments in full freedom and fluency in the Spirit. They are free in their thoughts to be totally focused on God and what He's doing. They've come a looong way! Here's the great news, we can do that on our local church level. The earth will be filled with glorious, anointed, and skilled music coming from the church!

Worship leaders have to be flexible to be moved by the Spirit. You can't be flexible if you have to think through every note or every chord change. I often hear worship leaders tell me they don't have time to practice. However, in order for you to attain and retain the skills necessary for the flexibility you need, you must find the time to practice. You don't have to find three hours all at once. Find fifteen minutes every day. The key is to exercise your gift every day. Even if you don't play an instrument, practice your voice. Practice your worship.

Flexibility is needed for different settings. Small group worship dynamics are different from large, corporate worship. In a smaller setting, use the framing model to place more emphasis on encountering God in intimate ways. Also, in small group settings, allow enough flexibility for people to bring their own contributions to the worship. They may bring a song or a Scripture. Use that to build off each other as the Spirit leads. Larger corporate settings often have more time constraints. Therefore, you have to plan your worship set more carefully to facilitate a sense of movement, progression, and resolution.

FIVE-PHASE MODEL

John Wimber used a five-phase model that generally works really well for me in a local church setting. There are other great models out there, but I've found this one works well for me. The five-phase model includes *celebration, exaltation, adoration, intimacy, and close out.* You will need to select songs for each of these phases that also keep your framing in mind.

Celebration is the first step of the five-phase model. Choose a song that is a call to worship. It's more of a horizontal song in which we sing to each other about God's greatness. It's a great way to gather people into a mindset of worship. On Sunday mornings, people will come in late, chat with their friends, and situate their children. They may have just come in from a facing a difficult situation or are carrying a heavy burden. There will be plenty of distractions. The celebration phase allows you to draw their attention to the service and call them into a posture of worship. I like to think of the celebration phase as embracing the room. You embrace the room in celebration and singing about God and giving thanks.

The second phase is *exaltation.* It's similar to the call to worship, but you begin to bring them more toward the Lord. You move them from a horizontal focus to a vertical gaze directly at God. Exaltation is like pointing your finger at God and saying, "Look! There He is! He's coming!" In the exaltation phase we sing songs about His beauty and greatness. You lift Him up.

The third phase is *adoration*. This is when we really pour out our love and devotion to God. You sing psalms to Him and your response to His love. The perspective shifts from singing about "Him" or "us" to "You" and "I."

Intimacy songs are the fourth phase, and they flow very naturally from the adoration phase. In the intimacy phase we speak directly to God and love directly on Him and allow Him to love on us. Depending on your setting, you can take the intimacy phase to different degrees. The focus is drawing near to God and He draws near to you. It's about the closeness.

The final phase of the five-phase model is *close out*. You bring everyone back to agreement in the close out. We agree with the encounter we just had, and we agree with what God is saying to us during worship. We claim the things He's spoken over us. It's the "amen" to the prayers offered up during the worship set. The close out may also be a precursor to the sermon topic if you know that ahead of time.

The biggest key to leading worship is to be the lead worshiper. We can't lead people into something we don't devote ourselves to as well. Each of these tools and techniques has helped me as I seek excellence in my worship leading, but each leader is unique. They may not work for you in your setting. I encourage you to try a variety of models and find what helps you connect best with the movement of the Spirit in the setting God has placed you.

CHAPTER 9

BASKING IN
THE GLORY

Layers of dimension define our experiences in worship. Thanksgiving, praise, and worship open the door to divine encounter and intimacy with God. They usher in the Presence. That's the first level. The second level is the anointing. When the anointing comes, power is released. The final dimension of worship is the glory. Worship, anointing, and glory are escalating dimensions of our experience of God. When the Presence comes, power (anointing) comes. When the power comes, the glory comes.

Revivalist Ruth Heflin stated it this way, "You praise until the spirit of worship comes. You worship until the spirit of glory comes, and then you stand in the glory."[1] We plow the ground of the glory with praise and worship. We till the environment until it's soft enough to receive the glory. Then when the glory comes, a harvest springs forth. The glory and the anointing work together in a two-punch. They are a two-edged sword. The anointing flows into the glory and the glory flows into the anointing.

The glory realm is where miracles occur. People are healed in the glory. Demons flee and lose their oppressive hold in the glory. People become whole when they stand in the glory. They are accelerated farther into their destiny. Problems, addictions, and issues that normally would have taken years to resolve are decimated in an instant. The future is brought into the present when the glory comes. In the glory, we touch Heaven, the place of no tears, no weeping, no sin, and no death. In the glory, God makes His home with us. It's Heaven on earth. I've tasted the glory, and I long to experience it again. It's what gets me out of bed every morning and excites me to the piano and to worship.

The glory is hard to define. It is best experienced. But we can describe it. Randy Clark gave me a book called *They Told Me Their Stories*. It is a compilation of biographical accounts from witnesses of the Azusa Street outpouring, which occurred at the beginning of the twentieth century. The people interviewed in the book were seniors at the time of the publication, but they had been children and teens at the time of the revival. The revival was marked by the presence of the "Shekinah glory" cloud that would rest upon the people. The individuals in the book described the glory as a tangible glowing cloud that would enter the building. At times it came as a fire on the building and coming from the building. There were reports of the fire department being contacted by witnesses concerned about flames leaping from the building.

Whenever the Shekinah glory came, miracles happened. Amputated limbs grew out. A withered woman on her deathbed was instantly healed and gained 40 pounds in a matter of hours. The children would play in the mist-like cloud and breathe in the sensation of pure oxygen. The glory would fall in the building, but its effects would ripple out. Passersby would fall out in the Spirit or speak in tongues for the first time or experience instantaneous healing without even being aware of what was happening inside the building.

That's the kind of glory I long for. It's Heaven—but it's now and it's on earth. I've never experienced it as strongly as described at Azusa Street, but I know I've tasted it. I've experienced God's presence and power in remarkable ways in the glory.

A few years ago, I witnessed The Call in Nashville, held in the Titans stadium. About 30,000 people gathered to pray and intercede in worship for our nation. Michael W. Smith was leading worship, and everyone was devoted to nothing but prayer and intercession. It was one of the most amazing, and definitely the largest, prayer meetings I had ever seen. One night, Ray Hughes brought in a group of 300 shofar players right in the middle of the stadium. The entire crowd of 30,000 shouted and the 300 shofars blew all at the same time. The sound was stunning and chilling. The sound I heard was greater than the sound coming from the voices and the shofars. There was another layer to the sound. It was a sound in the Spirit that was birthed out of the sound in the natural. It rumbled and reverberated.

Something opened up in the Spirit at that moment. It wasn't something that could be touched or manipulated or heard with the natural ears, but it was very real. It was a new dimension that hadn't been heard or accessed in many, many years. There was something very familiar about that sound, as if it were ancient and had remained silenced for centuries until that moment when our praise resurrected it.

Could you imagine what it would have been like to be someone walking past the stadium at that moment? It was a shout unlike any human sound; it was animated with living sound waves and frequencies. This was no touchdown shout. It was truly otherworldly. It was the sound of Heaven opening above us and dripping through the atmosphere into that region.

If the lost heard it, their spirits would have been activated. They would have recognized that sound as something special. They may not have acknowledged it or responded to it, but their spirits knew. We were all created in the glory, and our destiny is to return to that glory. Even the spirit of a lost person recognizes the sound of their birthplace. They are just one revelation away from knowing Christ, and if opening up the glory realm can give them that revelation, then it is worth every sacrifice made along the way.

When God shows up and the glory comes, everyone's attention is on Him. There are no distractions. No other earthly circumstance carries any significance next to His presence. When the glory comes, we are no longer in control. He is in control—not because He takes over our will but because our flesh bows to the glory of God, and His will is accomplished in us. Every eye is turned to God and every heart is eager with expectation of what God will do next. Every ear's hearing is magnified in anticipation of God's sound.

Psalm 97 speaks of the glory as a cloud that surrounds Him. It reminds me of the cloud described at Azusa Street. In this psalm all the people see His glory:

> *The Lord reigns; Let the earth rejoice;*
> *Let the multitude of isles be glad!*
> *Clouds and darkness surround Him;*
> *Righteousness and justice are*
> *the foundation of His throne.*
> *A fire goes before Him,*
> *And burns up His enemies round about.*
> *His lightnings light the world;*
> *The earth sees and trembles.*
> *The mountains melt like wax*
> *at the presence of the Lord,*
> *At the presence of the Lord of the whole earth.*
> *The heavens declare His righteousness,*
> *And all the peoples see His glory* (Psalm 97:1-6).

I want to participate in that kind of undeniable vision—when *all* people see His glory.

There are no formulas to create the glory. We open the door with worship, but we can't make the glory come. However, there are things we can do to create an environment in which God's presence can more easily come. I have discovered three keys to unlocking the glory: expectation, unity, and rest.

UNLOCKING THE GLORY

The first key to unlocking the glory is *expectation*. Sadly, many churches have a very low expectation level. They don't actually expect God to show up, so they never do anything to create a space for His glory to dwell. They are never disappointed because they don't expect anything to happen. However, they also never experience the anointing and the glory realm. I'd rather err on the side of expecting too much and seeing God move than expecting nothing and getting exactly what I hoped for.

We can't survive on church as normal. Sunday morning clock in and clock out won't cut it. It's as if we create these church machines so people can come and fulfill their religious duties, but no one ever expects God to actually come. That kind of atmosphere atrophies faith.

As worship leaders, we have to help our people exercise their faith muscles. Remind them that we expect God to do something amazing in the service. Recount stories about the glory. Sing songs of the mighty ways God comes and touches us. As we build an expectation for God to come, His presence is welcomed. As a culture of expectation is nurtured in the church, the congregation will begin to show excitement and anticipation for what God will do. Their hearts will already be turned toward Him, and the expectation will foster an environment for God to move.

The second key to unlocking the glory is *unity*. Agreement is a powerful weapon against doubt. Unity happens in two directions. First, we seek *vertical unity* with Heaven. When we come into agreement and alignment with Heaven, when we declare what Heaven is declaring, there is no separation between us. Heaven becomes open to us and envelopes all around us. Heaven is the place where God's glory dwells. So when we align ourselves with Heaven, we invite God's glory to rest upon us.

The second type of unity is *horizontal unity* with each other. We seek to be united with each other. That can happen musically when everyone comes together to the same note and same words. But even more significant than musical unison is spiritual unison. We declare together that we are opening a place for God's glory to rest. With one mind, one mouth, and one heart, we declare in unison that the Lord is good and His mercy endures forever. This reminds me of the passage from Second Chronicles in which the people set aside their divisions. Regardless of our divisions, we are going after God together.

You can practice this in your Sunday morning services. Make a unity declaration such as, "I know we have all come here with different opinions, philosophies, and maybe even different beliefs. But regardless of our divisions, we are all unified in purpose. We all want to touch God's heart this morning and we all seek to come into His presence. Let's put aside our differences and join together in worship to see what God will do. Let's press in together. Let's consecrate ourselves to Him and expect Him to do something amazing."

Bringing your people together in unity helps them also come into agreement and alignment with the order of Heaven. When we can get our congregation to agree, then God will manifest Himself in our meetings.

God loves to come to us when we are in unison, of one heart and one mind and devoted to one purpose: "Behold, how good and how pleasant it is for brethren to dwell together in unity!" (Psalm 133:1). God takes delight in our unity. He loves to respond to our unity. He can't help Himself but to answer the movements of hearts in unison toward Him. His glory is released in our unified declarations.

The trick is getting everyone on board. It can be daunting as a worship pastor to get everyone to focus on Him. There is always a fringe. A core group of worshipers can usually be counted on to be at the front of the stage, eager to worship. Then you have the majority of the congregation who may not be quite as excited, but they usually follow our leadership into a place of worship. But then there is the fringe. The fringe can be formidable.

Don't let the fringe intimidate you. Just move forward in your worship. We do our best, and let God handle the rest. God still loves to move even if there is a fringe. Remember that He loves the people in the fringe. He's a merciful God who likes to show off. The fringe won't hold Him back. Very seldom does every person participate in worship, and that's okay. You can have unity and have grace for the people who are not at that place yet. Trust that God will move even if not everyone follows where you sense the Spirit moving.

The third key to unlocking the glory is *rest*. The pressure is not on us to work up the glory. We can't make God show up. We can't make miracles occur. We can worship and submit to the Spirit's lead, but we can't make anything happen. So we just rest and join Heaven's symphony.

There's a temptation to work things up and up and up until we get to a place where the glory can come. But that's not how it happens. We don't work anything up. We just submit our hearts to worshiping God, and then we follow Him on the adventure He leads us on.

In fact, the less we work, the more we are able to get out of the way. The smaller we become, the more He shows up. It's a mystery. It takes all the pressure off us.

There are times we press in with our praise, but it's not with the goal in mind to make something happen. We press in simply to praise Him because He's worthy of praise. The goal is to set our affections on Him, not to make Him do something. We just worship Him because He is worthy to be worshiped. Then we step out of the way and just enjoy Him.

You can only enjoy God in a state of rest. You can't enjoy Him when you are striving to get to Him. Joy happens in rest. So when we worship and the glory comes, just rest. Sit in it. Enjoy it. Bask.

Bask in the glory! The glory is the place where Heaven meets earth. It's the answer to Jesus' prayer for God's will to be done on earth as it is in Heaven. When we are in an environment that is as it is in Heaven, there is no sickness, no pain, and no suffering.

We can access that realm by worshiping as it is in Heaven. When we step into Heaven's symphony and join in the chorus, we have stepped into the atmosphere of His glory. If you have a sickness in your body and you step into Heaven, your sickness leaves. So when the glory realm opens up here, the same thing happens. You don't have to do anything to be healed. You just step into it. The broken heart is instantly healed in the same way.

When we create an atmosphere that connects Heaven's sounds to earth, there is no limit to what can happen. I have witnessed it myself with increasing frequency and intensity. God wants to bring Heaven to earth. Earth is His footstool, and He loves to bring His glory here.

I think the reason He's releasing His glory more and more is because we have put our hand in the cookie jar, so to speak. We have pressed in through our worship and we've touched Heaven. He responds to that touch with an increase of His presence and glory.

I seek nothing more than to see Heaven come here on earth; for earth to be as it is in Heaven. I don't want to create anything or work anything up. I can't add anything to Heaven! So I simply seek to see God in His heavenly throne, to hear the heavenly sounds. I want to see and hear and touch so I can join. I touch Heaven and Heaven comes down. I join Heaven; then earth becomes as it is in Heaven. Heaven and earth become inseparable, and we are in the glory.

When in the glory, only one response remains—bask! So I encourage you, join the symphony! Become aware of His presence all around you: in nature, in Heaven, the symphony continues throughout eternity never ceasing before the throne. If you listen closely you can hear it everywhere! It's Heaven's symphony and all of us are the instruments!

ENDNOTE

1.   Ruth Ward Heflin, *Glory: Experiencing the Atmosphere of Heaven* (Hagerstown, MD: McDougal Publishing Company, 1996).

ABOUT STEVE SWANSON

Steve Swanson has traveled worldwide leading people in worship. He carries a powerful anointing and impartation in worship, intercession, and prophecy that creates an atmosphere of breakthrough in worship that opens the heavens. His unique gifting and passion allow worshipers to experience freedom, joy, and intimacy with the Lord. Steve has released 25 worship CDs and continues to record and produce his own as well as other artists' works.

Steve, his wife, Lisa, and their two sons reside in Casa Grande, Arizona. Since 1997 they have overseen Friends of the Bridegroom Worship Ministries, a ministry devoted to the release of His creativity in worship and the arts on the earth. In 2012 Steve and Lisa opened The Fourth Door Worship Arts Healing Center, a creative center dedicated toward worship art healing gatherings and training in Englewood, Florida.

CONTACT INFORMATION

www.steveswanson.org
1460 S. McCall Rd.
Suite 1E
Englewood, FL 34223
Telephone: 941-475-5060